M000274208

Rebuilding Shattered Worlds

....

Anthropology of Contemporary North America

SERIES EDITORS

James Bielo, *Miami University*

Carrie Lane, *California State University, Fullerton*

ADVISORY BOARD

Peter Benson, *Washington University in St. Louis*

John L. Caughey, *University of Maryland*

Alyshia Galvez, *Lehman College*

Carol Greenhouse, *Princeton University*

John Hartigan, *University of Texas*

John Jackson Jr., *University of Pennsylvania*

Ellen Lewin, *University of Iowa*

Bonnie McElhinny, *University of Toronto*

Shalini Shankar, *Northwestern University*

Carol Stack, *University of California, Berkeley*

Rebuilding Shattered Worlds

Creating Community by Voicing the Past

Andrea L. Smith and Anna Eisenstein

University of Nebraska Press
Lincoln and London

© 2016 by the Board of Regents of the University
of Nebraska

Parts of chapter 2 first appeared as "The Language of
'Blight' and Easton's 'Lebanese Town': Understanding a
Neighborhood's Loss to Urban Renewal" (with Rachel
Scarpato), in *Pennsylvania Magazine of History and
Biography* 134, no. 2 (2010): 127–64; parts of chapter 3
first appeared as "Thoroughly Mixed Yet Thoroughly
Ethnic: Indexing Class with Ethnonyms" (with Anna
Eisenstein), in *Journal of Linguistic Anthropology* 23,
no. 2 (2013): E1–22.

All rights reserved. Manufactured in the United
States of America ∞

Library of Congress Control Number: 2016948027

Set in ITC Charter by Rachel Gould.

Contents

Illustrations

Acknowledgments

Ethnographic research is possible only through the generosity of others, and because this study spanned nearly ten years, a large number of people are owed our deepest gratitude. From the community members suggesting research topics and meeting with us at length, to the student participants signing up for a class, to the college administrators and colleagues who supported the project with funding and by approving new courses: we are grateful for people's enthusiastic engagement with us across so many years of research.

We first acknowledge community members who provided early direction, including Jane Moyer of the Northampton Historical Society, who met us on many occasions; and Deacon Anthony Koury from Our Lady of Lebanon Maronite Catholic Church, who introduced us to key former neighborhood residents. Reverend Sue Ruggles of the St. John's Evangelical Lutheran Church masterminded the initial Taylor School reunion and shared with us address lists that allowed us to reach beyond Lebanese neighbors to a wider world of former neighbors. St. John's hosted our reunions and student scanning and interview sessions for years, and Pastor Ruggles often greeted our participants with words of welcome. Patsy Woodson and Norma Rosner worked behind the scenes, setting aside the vital meeting space. Barbara Kowitz of the Sigal Museum helped us find funding and hosted two large end-of-the-year parties for students, participants, and the wider community.

Our project never would have taken the direction it did had it not been for George Bright, then associate athletic director at Lafayette College; his grandfather plays an important role in the story told here. An Easton native, George knew potential speakers well and handpicked, it seemed to us later, the very best interlocutors we could imagine. This project would have been very different had George not been willing to meet with us, at length, that fateful day in 2010.

Most of all, we thank the participants, who shared with us their stories, photos, and memories of their former neighborhood and its demolition, especially Robert Apgar Sr., Ronald Apgar, Gloria Armstrong, Mary Azzalina, Lois Bachman, Sadie Bader, JoEllen Bartolacci, George Baurkot, Marlene Bedway, Katherine Benton, Jim Canone, Oscar Canone, Ralph Cianci, Diane Coker, Beverly Cook, Charmaine Crouse, H. Robert Daws, Mary Alice Delk, Marion Estephan, Eva Farhat, Sadie Ferreira, Carol Free, Doreen Free, David Freytag, Frank A. Galasso, Frank J. Galasso, Mary Galasso, Gina Germano, Irene Gilbert, Vincent Gioieni, Don Hicks, Raymond Hunt, George Jabbour, Sharon John, Annie Jones, Roseann Joseph, Beverly Karam, Yasmine Karam, Frances Ketchen, Pete Keyser, William Keyser, Katie Kmetz, Barbara Miller, Terry Langen, Tony Lisinichia, Charlene Loprete, Donald Miller, Verna Miller, Patricia Morris, Ross Oliver, Agnes Pellicotti, Perry Pellicotti, Carolyn Pokrivchak, Verna Piraino, Joan Price, Mita Prime, Herbert Robinson, Clifford Rose, William Sanderson, Carmelo Saveri, Norman Seidel, Livingston Smith, John Squarcia, John Thomas, Josephine Thomas, Vita Torcivia, Sam Vilari, and Folee Williams. We'd like to give special thanks to members of the reunion organizing committee: Len Buscemi, James Edwards, Maddie Hannah, Mary Pleiss, Vivian Richetta, John and Sonja Shaheen, Bob Simons, Bob and Rosemary Smith, Carl Taylor, and Melvin Taylor. We will be forever grateful for their willingness to meet with us regularly to plan the reunions and to serve as subjects for student interviews. Their stories of life in Easton continue to influence how we see our town.

An early version of chapter 4 was presented at the panel "Strategies and Performances of Temporal Heteroglossia," co-organized by Jacqueline Messing and Andrea Smith and held at the 2013 annual meeting of the American Anthropological Association. We thank Jacqui and fellow panelists Evelyn Dean-Olmsted, Aurora Donzelli, Adam Harr, Sarah Hillewaert, Marco Jacquemet, Patricia Lange, Kathe Managan, Julia McKinney, Ashley Stinnett, and Camilla Vasquez for their engaging and insightful comments. This presentation was preceded by an earlier version presented at the panel "Voices Inside Voices Inside Voices: Interpreting Multivocality," organized at the 2012 Oral History Association annual meeting by Henry Greenspan. We thank Hank and fellow panelists Susan Clemens-Bruder, Amy Kesselman, and Judy Ridner for their suggestions.

From Andrea:

I first recognize the many talented students who worked on different facets of this project since its inception. Eduardo Sanchez and James Sommers undertook independent studies with me that led downtown, and Marvin Snipes, Amy Spooner, and Rachel Scarpato carried out pilot projects as a Mellon-funded "Community of Scholars" in 2006–7. Rachel Scarpato worked on this full-time in the summer of 2007, and I will never forget how much fun we had sleuthing in city archives. She conducted expert interviews with many of the early consultants, and is thus partly responsible for the project's initial direction. Together we wrote the article "The Languages of Blight," on which chapter 2 is based. Kelsey Boyd, Walter Burkat, Emily Mulford, and Molly Leech were exemplary research assistants. Whole classes of students in my research methods seminar, A&S 244, carried out further interviews, culminating in a community-directed, student-authored book of neighborhood memories that students presented to their consultants at the end of the term. Finally, this book would never have been written without the amazing partnership with Anna, who stayed with the project for all four years of college while developing her own interests and during the first grueling years of graduate school. John Meier, of the Provost's Office, was always able to find ways to continue funding student research through the Lafayette Excel Scholars Program.

Several of the images are due to the efforts of Eric Luhrs, digital librarian at Lafayette's Skillman Library. He supported the creation of a digital map of the neighborhood, which involved lengthy scanning sessions carried out expertly by Paul Miller, also of the library. Amy Abruzzi first suggested this digital component. Diane Shaw of Skillman Library Special Collections helped us find sources. The maps are courtesy of our library's GIS and cartography whiz, John Clark, and illustrations drawn by Kristin Leader.

The project has benefited throughout from the support of department heads Howard Schneiderman, Dave Shulman, and Bill Bissell. Susan Niles was the first to suggest that I turn this project into a full-fledged course, and Dan Bauer's "tech clinics" provided me with a model of just how that might work. Alison Alexy's students in her research methods class collected early transcripts. Rebecca Kissane, herself a housing policy expert, suggested sources early on regarding urban renewal, and Caroline Lee took the time to provide comments on early drafts and suggested ways it could become a project about memory.

Finally, I thank my family for being there throughout.

From Anna:

Professor Smith's wonderful mentorship has defined my ability to contribute to this project, as well as my broader introduction to anthropology. As our writing and thinking continued beyond our shared time at Lafayette, and into my time at the University of Virginia, Ira Bashkow provided incisive comments on various drafts, as well as his consistent support. I thank members of the UVA Linguistic Anthropology Seminar in the fall of 2013 for feedback on an early version of what is now chapter 4. Many of the ideas in chapter 5 first began to develop during Adria LaViolette's course, Archaeology of Everyday Life, that same semester. And thanks to Nathan Hedges and Arsalan Khan for helpful conversations. My family, too, has been part of this project all along by way of constant encouragement.

Terminology and Transcription Conventions

Much of this book concerns a former way of speaking. Our speakers use many different and sometimes old-fashioned-sounding ethnic labels when describing each other or the neighborhood, for example, "Syrian" for Lebanese immigrants and "Afro-American" for black people, a practice we discuss at length in the chapters that follow. "Syrian Town" is used as a place-name even though it is a misnomer: the people about whom we write are Lebanese. Throughout the text, we continue to use our speakers' archaic terms, introducing them with quotation marks at first. The reader should keep this in mind and imagine quotation marks throughout the text. Where we do use quotation marks subsequently, it is to indicate particular instances of usage.

This work includes extensive excerpts from audiotaped interviews. We use the following transcription conventions:

. . .	pause in speech
—	sudden break in speech, usually to indicate that the speaker has changed topic midsentence
<u>word</u>	speaker's emphasis
word	authors' emphasis
[ ]	information provided by the authors

Rebuilding Shattered Worlds

1. Ethnography of the Expelled

In a small city in eastern Pennsylvania, elderly men and women have been gathering to talk about the past. Ostensibly planned as elementary school reunions, these meetings allow participants to recollect a whole neighborhood. We have been following this activity since 2007; this book is the result of this inquiry.

What makes this reunion activity especially intriguing is the fact that the neighborhood these men and women are so keen to discuss is completely gone: it was obliterated during 1960s urban renewal projects. Many of the eighty- and ninety-year-olds meeting up in the dingy basement social hall are encountering each other for the first time since they were "scattered" by the demolitions. Now, a half-century after wrecking balls "took the heart out of the city," as one speaker puts it, they are reuniting to reminisce about the past. What is prompting them to meet, to meet here, and to meet now?

This is a study of memory and place, of place-loss and recovery. The effects of midcentury urban renewal on minority communities and urban landscapes are well documented in studies focusing on the nation's largest cities, such as Chicago, Boston, and Detroit.[1] Less examined have been the smaller cities, which also took advantage of generous federal funds to remove so-called blighted landscapes. This ethnographic study, conducted a half-century after renewal struck Easton, Pennsylvania, explores the ways a demolished neighborhood continues to reverberate in the imaginations of its former residents. This neighborhood, once known locally as "Syrian Town," was densely packed and inhabited by Lebanese Americans, Italian Americans, and African Americans, among others, and was noteworthy for its unusually integrated nature. Our book follows neighborhood reunions and the intersecting languages of blight, race, and place as elderly interlocutors attempt to make sense of the world they have lost.

This is an ethnography of *remembering*. Our speakers reconstruct Syrian Town through narratives of everyday life, elucidating the subjective experience of displacement in their own words. The power of place and the pull of former ways of speaking are two themes that run through this text. The unique circumstances of this study, in which people often meet for the first time since the neighborhood's destruction, provide a rare opportunity to observe the articulation of shared memories, a "collective memory" in the making. Although many of the reunion participants do not share identical life experiences, they nevertheless experience what appears to be a remarkable bonding as they reunite over smaller details that stem from having shared a common place, language, and class position within the wider cityscape. By following their gatherings, we are able to bring insights from linguistic anthropology on the role language plays in signaling the past and new work on materiality and memory together with a processual understanding of place to show how people collaboratively reconstruct their lost world in terms from a former era.[2] By conceptualizing historical consciousness as a form of "distributed cognition," we show how in collaborative collective remembering, linguistic terms and material objects serve as "signs of history," verbal and material clues to a lost world necessary for further recollecting.[3]

Urban Renewal as Place-Loss: Origins of This Project

The first glimpse of this book project occurred in 2006 when I heard back from a student I had sent to a local bar the night before. "Professor!" he exclaimed, animated when we met. "There really is a Lebanese night, and boy, are they mad! They are still talking about it is if it all happened yesterday!" The "they" Eddie encountered was a group of local Eastonians of Lebanese descent who met weekly at a local bar, Sami's Place, which had been moved to College Hill from the downtown neighborhood when it was seized by the city through eminent domain in 1965.[4] The "college" of College Hill is Lafayette College, a small private college known for its liberal arts and engineering focus that is situated on a bluff overlooking the city of thirty thousand. It is where I have been teaching anthropology since 1999. I followed up on Eddie's adventure and found, like he had, a vivacious group of friends, still seething about the effects "redevelopment" had on their lives.

In 2006 I had been seeking topics for student research related to local sites of memory: I had envisioned a series of research projects around monuments and commemorative plaques that students in my Social Memory seminar might pursue. A ninety-five-year-old head librarian at the county historical society suggested a different kind of "site of memory," a whole neighborhood lost to urban renewal. I was fascinated by librarian Jane Godfrey's accounts of the ethnic and racial mixture and harmony characterizing Syrian Town, and I had sent Eddie and a few other early student researchers to see if anyone was left who remembered what it had been like.

Preliminary research with members of the remaining local Lebanese community was astounding, and I was hooked. This community and its predicament compelled me, because the consequences of place-loss have been a topic of enduring interest, an interest that first led me to fieldwork among former settlers of Algeria. After their mass flight from Algeria to France at the end of the French-Algerian War in 1962, many former settlers (*pied-noirs*) spent much of their adult lives longing for the former colony. Not only did Algeria seem off-limits to them following the violence of the war, but also the country has undergone so many changes since decolonization as to become a different place from that imagined in their nostalgic yearnings.[5] As a result, settlers have developed a rich set of cultural creations, such as social clubs, genealogical societies, and an array of publications, that can be viewed, ultimately, as efforts to cope with place-loss. These creations include the Maltese settler clubs I studied that replaced journeys to the former colony with "return" trips to a prior homeland, Malta, and ongoing settler efforts to alter the French metropolitan landscape with the addition of monuments of or from the colony.[6]

"Place-loss," the removal from home, from a homeland, a severing from the source of an individual's foundational orienting sensory inputs—of smells, sounds, and material matrix—might be productively viewed across instances as a single phenomenon. The loss of place can be such a powerful motivating force that it can lead to a rewriting of history. When I explored the longing of Mormon settlers for their former hamlet of Forestdale, Arizona, I found an elaborate reworking of the late nineteenth-century past. Although documentary evidence indicates that the Mormon settlement of Forestdale was an example of squatters attempting to claim lands granted to the Western Apache as part of the White Mountain Apache Reservation, descendants of these early settler-squatters continue to discuss this place and their removal from it by federal officials as an unjust eviction. The careful retracing of village homesteads and their preservation in local lore and family history volumes demonstrate how expulsion and place-loss can be a powerful force that can endure, motivating creative production.[7]

As quickly became apparent, people were also coping with dramatic place-loss right in the Pennsylvania town where I teach and reside. But in contrast to the previous cases I have studied, the Eastonians I met were not removed from their homes; instead, their homes were removed from them. While some of the people discussed in this book live in virtually the same spatial coordinates as they had before, the land has been utterly transformed. This is certainly the case for many of the very old who live in senior citizen high-rises built on land seized through redevelopment and now look out on the contemporary wasteland that had once been their childhood home. While they have not crossed oceans or endured a dramatic regime change, their lived experiences and daily outlook echo those of the Maltese settlers I worked with who were ever-distracted by their memories of a former place and time.

After Eddie's providential adventure, undergraduates carried out further research in the spring of 2007. Rachel Scarpato continued to work with me that summer, and we investigated the history of the renewal project, culminating in a publication that forms the basis of a chapter in this book.[8] Anna Eisenstein, then an undergraduate as well, joined the project in 2009. The more we explored, the more we found a community fascinating to work with and fascinated by the idea of working with us. As they taught us, place-loss experienced through urban renewal is parallel in many ways to that stemming from emigration, diaspora, and the global sea change that was decolonization. Parallel though they are, the particular qualities of place-loss through urban renewal merit in-depth consideration.

FIG. I. A "nonplace" at the intersection of 4th and Ferry Streets. The gate on the left once encircled the Taylor School; it is now a church parking lot. The building on the right is one of the few buildings remaining from the neighborhood; it housed the Northampton Historical Society. Image courtesy of Andrea Smith.

Expulsion as American Leitmotif

In her recent book, *Expulsions: Brutality and Complexity in the Global Economy*, sociologist Saskia Sassen identifies expulsion as a leitmotif of the contemporary world order. She points to the sharp growth "in the number of people, enterprises, and places expelled from the core social and economic orders of our time." A new "logic of expulsion" is emerging, she writes, whether it be "expulsion from a life space" for people relegated to the lower levels of a world characterized by increasing inequality, extreme environmental devastation ("an expulsion of bits of life itself from the biosphere"), mass incarceration, or mass displacement due to war and disease. Drawing on cases from across the globe, she writes that "since the 1980s, there has been a strengthening of dynamics that expel people from the economy and from society, and these dynamics are now hardwired into the normal functioning of these spheres."[9]

Our work speaks to the lengthy genealogy of expulsion in the United States specifically. This trend has deep roots, as evidenced by the case at hand. Syrian Town was located in the heart of the city and bordered the railroad station. This area, composed of row houses, single-family residences, and independent shops, was eradicated in short order despite clear local opposition, and its residents were expelled. Today, it is a "non-place" typical of supermodernity, an expanse of empty parking lots, a worn motel, and federal offices typically devoid of people, except for a few solitary older people struggling to bring their purchases back to their apartments.[10]

The eradication of a small neighborhood in a small city in Pennsylvania was not unusual for the time, for the 1950s and 1960s were decades of demolition. Title 1 of the Housing Act of 1949 provided funding to cities, allowing them to purchase properties through eminent domain with the hope of encouraging redevelopment on cleared lands. City upon city took advantage of this and successor programs, altering urban America to a staggering degree. Projects often fell short of expectations, however, and local redevelopment organizations did not always comply with federal requirements to replace demolished housing with additional housing units, exacerbating existing housing shortages for lower-income families.[11] Cities often practiced "bulldozer" renewal, eradicating whole neighborhoods. Projects sometimes proceeded despite civic outcry, and in city after city, cleared lands remained vacant. Mark Gelfand observed, "Throughout the country, wrecking crews leveled the homes and businesses of urban Americans, who then watched their former properties sprout weeds and remain fallow for years."[12] Even smaller cities like Easton, Pennsylvania, with a population of approximately thirty-five thousand in the 1950s, sought these funds. In fact, by 1961, almost 28 percent of cities of twenty-five thousand to fifty thousand inhabitants were participating in federally funded renewal projects.[13] Expulsion was in vogue and continues to this day; Americans everywhere cope with its aftermath.

Twentieth-century urban renewal episodes, however, are but a recent iteration of an American leitmotif of longue durée. A settler society, this country has a history of relentless uprooting and replacement of populations through a continual shuffling of people westward, eastward, and northward, disruptions that help feed an ever-evolving class hierarchy.

Similar if not identical processes are ongoing today, even in this small city: Easton leaders, while critical of the way urban renewal was carried out in the 1960s, continue to tap federal funds to tear down and rebuild now-defunct businesses on the very lands cleared earlier; a bus depot is now under construction. It is thus vitally important to understand the causes and consequences of the "logic of expulsion" that pervades contemporary American society.

The scholarship on postwar urban renewal has rightly highlighted the nation's larger cities, such as Atlanta, Boston, Philadelphia, Chicago, Kansas City, New York, and Newark.[14] As a result, however, experiences in smaller cities remain a "largely unexamined component of our recent history."[15] Furthermore, citywide studies often emphasize the whole picture at the expense of subjective experiences. Our study starts in the opposite direction and emphasizes an understudied dimension of renewal, namely, its long-term effects on specific individuals. How does the renewal experience compare to other well-studied examples of expulsion or diaspora? Former colonists can unite around images, songs, histories, and maps, the whole ideological underpinnings of a former sociopolitical order. Armenians living in Canada today display pictures of Mount Ararat in their homes.[16] But in Syrian Town, everyday life has carried on almost exactly as before. In such a case, what are the resources people use to reconstruct or return to past worlds? We will want to consider which signs and symbols they mobilize and to what ends. The role played by language and narrative and by material culture—or its near-complete absence—in influencing people's ways of remembering are all concerns that motivated this research. Through this focus, we want to emphasize the place-loss generated by the urban renewal fever that has been sweeping this country in waves since its earliest years, accelerating in speed and scale since the 1950s. Whole neighborhoods were forever changed, whole city landscapes were completely reworked, and the social consequences have been catastrophic.

Informed by new literature in the anthropology of space and materiality, we explore the subjective meanings associated with a rapid loss of place, focusing on how that place-loss reverberates decades after the fact, creating such a powerful affective force that it may, paradoxically, help to unite people years later.

Bridging Divides

On a hot day in late July 2010, we held an elementary school reunion in Easton, Pennsylvania, in the basement of a downtown Lutheran church. The atmosphere was abuzz with anticipation; participants were drawn by the possibility of meeting former school friends and neighbors, many of whom they hadn't seen for fifty years. When we pulled into the parking lot, Jerry, an eighty-five-year-old black man bedecked in jacket and embroidered cap, called out happily, "Here are the instigators!" as he came to greet us. Inside waited Sal, a self-described "Italian" of Sicilian ancestry who was also attired formally. As we came down the stairs hauling a wooden stand and poster board we brought to decorate the drab basement meeting space, he announced his age, ninety-two, to the youngest of the organizers, winking as he added, "And I am not senile."

As people arrived, we directed them to displays of photographs we brought depicting street scenes of another era and eventually to a sea of folding metal tables and chairs that filled the vast room. The din was great as approximately thirty people gathered and multiple conversations proceeded simultaneously, and we wondered if people would be able to connect across the many divides separating them. As the event commenced, one octogenarian suggested that we go around the room introducing everyone by name, former street address, and years at the school. For the women, it was essential to declare (loudly) their maiden name. At that point, other people often shouted out street names or siblings' nicknames before the speaker could: "Ah, Bank and South 5th!" Recognition proceeded according to people's former location within the place they were remembering. If there was any segregation at this event, it was by age as people sat along three long tables. Gloria, a spunky woman of German and English descent in her eighties, joked with a black man, Mark, who was nicely dressed in a bright gold blazer. He called her his "girlfriend." A small group of men of various races and ethnicities (black, Lebanese, Sicilian) talked at length about town movie theaters ("The Boyd The-a-tre!" "The Ranch House!") and which street barricades they could get through when chased by the local police.

This was the first of a half-dozen reunions we held and one of dozens of monthly meetings organized since 2007. Why are elderly former res-

FIG. 2. Introductions at a reunion. Image courtesy of Carl Taylor.

idents of a small neighborhood demolished in the 1960s so eager to
gather and reminisce about past times? Is there something unique about
Easton's Syrian Town neighborhood worth reporting today? We provide
more details about the reunion functions below, but first, we introduce
the key theoretical axes along which this text contributes. By foregrounding local discourses of Syrian Town belonging, our work offers an account
of the local boundary lines around race, class, and ethnic categories.
Woven into those local identity categories is the importance of spatial
boundaries and physical structures; people's relationships to the material elements of the Syrian Town neighborhood prove central to their
membership in the in-group of rememberers. Thus, we find it useful to
conceptualize place as a process that both shapes and reflects social
groups and power dynamics between them. Crucially, our interlocutors'
insights about their world became accessible to us when we attended
closely to the ways they talked about it. Our approach, then, is one that
privileges close attention to our speakers' words and phrases and how
specific linguistic practices participate in the work of remembering,
alongside other material processes of signification.[17]

Articulating Difference: Local Dialogues
on Race, Class, and Ethnicity

Syrian Town was located just off the city center. Its toponym identifies it as an "ethnic" part of town; clearly, with this appellation, the neighborhood was known to be where the so-called Syrians lived (in this case, Christian Lebanese of the Maronite faith from what is now Lebanon). John Hartigan Jr. has observed that racial designations of places are often a gross simplification: "Neighborhoods are considered—by insiders and outsiders—to be 'white' or 'Black' according to shifting criteria, but the designation almost always masks the inevitable degrees of racial heterogeneity in any one location."[18] The same pattern holds true for neighborhoods granted *ethnic* designations. In Easton, the "Syrian" label masked the neighborhood's actual racial and ethnic diversity. At the time of the demolitions, it was not even *majority* Lebanese: by our calculations, based on the 1963 city directory for the streets concerned in the immediate renewal area, 20 percent of the households were Lebanese American, 25 percent were Italian American, and 30 percent were African American, with the remaining 25 percent of Irish, Greek, Pennsylvania Dutch, English, and other extractions described by our interviewees as "Americans."[19] Most neighborhood blocks had residents of each of these backgrounds living side by side.

When we spoke with former residents, it was not the Lebaneseness of the neighborhood that people found noteworthy but its racial and ethnic *mixture*. We noted this emphasis on diversity right away in the ways our interlocutors described this place, characterizations they volunteered without any prompting on our part. Octogenarian Agatha, of Lebanese descent, regularly identified people as members of one of several distinct ethnic groups. As she explained, "In those days, the Lebanese, the Jews, the Italians, the Afro-Americans . . . all lived *mixed*, one right after the other." The integrated nature of the neighborhood's businesses was a feature that local historian and nearly century-old Jane Godfrey remembered when she suggested that we research this past. At length she described "taverns" run by Lebanese women that catered to the local African Americans, as well as to the Lebanese. Thus, while businesses were known to be "Lebanese," "Italian," or "Afro-American," they attracted a pluralistic clientele. Agatha noted a similar phenomenon: "There was an African American poolroom on Bank Street, South Bank Street—there was a poolroom there. And it was a hanging place for the Lebanese, Italians, the Afro-Americans, and the Jewish—they all used to get together."

"Italian," "Lebanese," "German." Our speakers of all backgrounds described themselves and each other in this way, using a vernacular we explicate in chapter 3. It is noteworthy that people of these backgrounds never employed the label "white." The very persistence of *ethnic* labels in our speakers' speech and the concomitant absence of overtly racialized language are significant patterns that call into question a dominant narrative of the relationship of ethnicity to race and whiteness in the contemporary United States. Many scholars in U.S. immigration history and whiteness studies argue that people of recent European immigrant backgrounds began to view themselves less as members of distinct ethnic groups and more in racial terms by the middle of the twentieth century: Chicago by the 1920s, Philadelphia by the 1930s and 1940s.[20] This development and the related emergence of a white racial identity are often associated with the "new racial alchemy" created by migrations of African Americans from the South and subsequent competition over resources, especially housing.[21] According to this perspective, immigrants or their descendants adopted the prevailing national racial classification scheme rooted in a black/white binary, moving from "Irish" (or "Italian," "Jewish," etc.) to "white," a process some have termed "Americanization through racism."[22]

Our findings directly challenge this master narrative and suggest that racial constructions are highly variable and localized. As Hartigan argues, "Racial identities are produced and experienced distinctly in different locations, shaped by dynamics that are not yet fully comprehended."[23] One of the goals of this book, then, is to take seriously the stories told by our speakers—their content, themes, and the language used in their telling—and ask what deeper meanings they are urgently communicating to us. Was Syrian Town a different kind of place? In what ways and how did it become so? Since reflections on the past often carry an implicit commentary on the present, we ask what messages our speakers are directly and indirectly relaying about the contemporary moment. Was a racially segregated and highly racialized America inevitable?

A starting point for addressing these questions is to begin with the Lebanese character of the neighborhood, exemplified by its toponym. Contemplating a *Lebanese* neighborhood already presents an important corrective to the dominant European-immigrant-to-white model, for no matter how they are described, Lebanese immigrants were not Europeans. Arabic-speaking immigrants had been coming to the United States from its earliest years, with noteworthy immigration from areas of the Ottoman Empire starting in the mid-1860s. Before 1899, legal nomenclature was highly variable.[24] Eventually, immigrants from the then Syrian Province of the Ottoman Empire, like Easton's Lebanese, were designated "Syrians."[25] This migration was predominantly composed of Christians of three Eastern Rite sects: Maronite, Orthodox, and Melkite Christians.[26]

By 1910 people labeled "Syrians" were found in all states, with populations concentrated in New York; Detroit; Boston; Providence, Rhode Island; and Worchester, Massachusetts. By the 1920s, neighborhoods with high concentrations of Syrian immigrants in U.S. cities were often identified as "Little Syria" or "Syrian Town."[27] Like other Arabic speakers, "Syrians" were often racialized and subject to suspicion in the nineteenth century. While legally redefined as "white" by a 1915 court case, anti-Syrian discrimination persisted across the nation for several more decades, as historians report from locations as far afield as Birmingham, Alabama, and North Dakota and as our speakers outlined.[28] Most of these neighborhoods, like Easton's Syrian Town, were leveled through urban renewal projects, and the only way to understand their characteristics is through historical reconstruction.

Like many other similarly named neighborhoods, Easton's Syrian Town was not exclusively Lebanese but multiethnic and multiracial. People identified today as blacks and whites lived side by side and frequented each other's shops. Reminiscences of Syrian Town, then, with stories of the neighborhood's interlocking mixture of Italians, Lebanese, Germans, blacks, and Irish, offer a rare glimpse not only into a neighborhood noted for its Lebaneseness but also into the dynamics of one of the country's few truly integrated northern neighborhoods.[29]

Place as Process

After overlooking space or considering it a backdrop, a fixed location upon which "culture" happened, the anthropology of space takes up its "production" directly.[30] A single landscape can be "multilocal," and multiple meanings associated with places are contested and change.[31] As we will show, in the early 1960s, conflicting notions of the meanings of Syrian Town confronted each other head-on, with one side winning all. This case reminds us that the production of space is always a political process and that place-making processes are not isolated from but best understood in relation to prevailing power struggles.[32]

Scholarship on place making is situated on a continuum between studies focused on space as symbol and reflection of social relations and works grounded in place making's very materiality.[33] We find most useful works that focus on both the "objective and relational properties and processes" and that draw inspiration from material studies scholarship, which endeavors to overcome the "mind-matter duality" by emphasizing *process* and *practice* and the development of the individual within a specific social and material milieu.[34] Space thus can be seen as a resource or ground for social relations, as well as a product of those same relations.[35] Social practices are key in this view, as they intervene between the subject and object worlds.[36] As Fred Myers puts it, "place-making" is not the projection of "pre-existing cultural templates on to a tabula rasa world, but a dialectical engagement of social and historical schemas of practical activity with worldly circumstance."[37]

One of the hallmarks of new works on materiality and place is the understanding that people and places are mutually constituted. Geographer Allan Pred's theory of "place as historically contingent process" provides a useful foundation for conceptualizing subjectivity, place, language, and objects together in a dynamic, diachronic perspective. Rather than viewing place as a backdrop for social life, the "structuring of space" is considered inseparable from the structuring of society. In his view, the "production of history, the becoming of places and the formation of biographies are enwrapped in one another" and viewed as inseparable from human practice, power relations, and knowledge.[38]

Pred proposes the concepts of "path" and "project" to help conceptualize a dynamic field that involves multiple, intersecting, and mutually interacting variables over time. "Path" refers to the "actions and events consecutively making up the existence of the individual," which has temporal and spatial attributes. The biography of a person then can be conceptualized as "an unbroken continuous path through time-space." We can conceptualize the biographies of other living things and human-made objects in the same way. The "project" is the series of tasks required to complete goal-oriented behaviors and in this framework involves the "coupling together in time and space of the uninterrupted paths of two or more people" along with tangible inputs such as buildings, tools, and so forth. In the process of carrying out projects, place is worked upon and changed, just as the human involved in such projects evolves and changes, leading to "detailed increments to his or her biography."[39] People's paths and their engagement in collective projects are not wide open but limited by a variety of "constraints," including the availability and competition over resources, the fact that people cannot be in two places at the same time, and constraints related to power.

Language appears in Pred's model as both constraint and enabling condition, for it is a necessary medium that allows people to cooperate in any given area while being constantly changed by these very actions: "Language is always *becoming* in the sense that its components are either very gradually and unintentionally altered through daily use in stable and recurrent institutional projects or incrementally and sometimes radically changed through the introduction, abandonment or modification of institutional projects and their associated path-coupling requirements."[40] Language too has a "biography," one integrally connected to the daily projects or practices people undertake as they engage with the material world and each other. We will be foregrounding this evolution of language-in-space over the course of this book.

The people who gather to discuss Syrian Town can be seen as having traveled along intersecting or parallel "paths" with biographies that connected at some point at the same place. Sometimes individuals engaged in solo "paths" across the same space. Since we can conceive of the biographies of buildings and streetscapes in the same way, we can argue that each of the individuals in our study had paths that intersected for some stretch of time with those of the material components of the city. Mikhail

Bakhtin's notion of the chronotope (literally, "time-space," a literary device found in the novel form) will become useful as we consider the ways traveling along similar "paths" and thus coexisting in the same space-time continuum influence speech; we explain our use of this concept more fully in the chapters that follow.[41] Individuals were also engaged in collective activities or Pred's "projects" when their "paths" intersected during such activities as "walking to school" with siblings or others, "running an errand," or engaging in a more elaborate, fully orchestrated collective project such as "attending school," "going to the movies," or "working together" at a factory job.

Archaeologist Julia Hendon helpfully extends Pred's notion of project to consider the people engaged together in a project as a "community of practice," a phrase that calls attention to the physicality of collective endeavors. Her research focuses on households and the communities of practice related to production and reproduction in indigenous communities of a thousand years ago in what is now Honduras. She considers the role of *objects* in these practices, writing that "objects afford possibilities for action and meaning making that interact with the physical properties and capabilities of the human body and its sensory apparatus." Just as carrying out "projects" with various tools results in changes in these tools, other objects, places, and even people, as in Pred's model, Hendon discusses the dialectical relationship between objects and bodies, exploring, for instance, how the manipulation of stone metates requires a certain way of sitting and moving that, over time, literally alters the user's physical form. She focuses on the physicality of craft making and how people engaged in these activities are laying down similar "body memories" as "subjectivity and materiality come together."[42]

Our study is in many ways the mirror image of an archaeological study like Hendon's: she starts with material objects people have left behind and from them reconstructs the communities of practice they suggest or index. Our study works in the opposite direction. Starting from stories told us by living people about places and practices now obliterated, we try to reconstruct the missing objects and places through their memories and stories. As we will demonstrate, because of the integration of subjectivity and materiality, this reconstruction not only is feasible but often appears to be a cathartic activity for our speakers.

Igor Kopytoff has emphasized the "life-histories of artefacts," and this insight has led material studies scholars to explore the ways "memory and awareness of the past is associated with things: things have histories, and the memory of that particular history is evoked by and carried with the thing itself."[43] As a result, the "affective power of the artefact can continue, by virtue of that history, to exist in the present."[44] There is value in considering an individual's biography in conjunction with his or her language biography, as well as the biography of a place, the biographies of its material components, and the biographies of objects.[45] When we view subjectivity in this way we can better understand why there would be long-standing repercussions for people when the life of a place is terminated, when people find themselves removed from cherished objects or revel in touching again an old-style automobile.

From Social Memory to Remembering

In what ways do people dispersed from a place reconnect across temporal and spatial divides? One way to approach this question might be to presume a "collective memory" that binds the individuals together. Indeed, this is how we initially conceived of our study. This concept, from Durkheim disciple Maurice Halbwachs, is often the starting point for any discussion of a common historical consciousness. Halbwachs posited the existence of "collective frameworks of memory," the "instruments used by the collective memory to reconstruct an image of the past which is in accord, in each epoch, with the predominant thoughts of the society." He argued that individual recollection is possible *only* in relation to the "collective memory" and "social frameworks" of memory: "It is to the degree that our individual thought places itself in these frameworks and participates in this memory that it is capable of the act of recollection."[46]

Since Halbwachs, many scholars have explored the cultural memory of smaller societal subgroups, conceptualizing an amorphous society-wide "collective memory" as composed of smaller "memory communities" organized around such characteristics as racial, class, or gender distinctions. Iwona Irwin-Zarecka conceptualizes these as "communities of memory," communities with distinct orientations to the past.[47] Sensitive to power dynamics and the political uses of the past, many anthropologists explore how the past can serve political movements and forge imagined national communities.[48] They also study the relationship between dominant and popular perspectives and their interaction within a "public theatre of history."[49]

Following this logic to an exploration of a multiethnic neighborhood, one might posit distinct ethnic "memory communities," each with its own version of neighborhood life, its silenced stories, and its private celebrations. Originally, we anticipated applying this perspective to the fallout of Syrian Town: we thought that because residents are now scattered into more homogeneous racial or religion-based enclaves, stories of neighborhood life might exhibit some distinct patterning along ethnic lines. We imagined that the nostalgia-imbued tales of interracial harmony that we first heard from residents of Lebanese origin might be challenged by their African American counterparts.[50] What we found instead was different: not only were the stories similar in tone and content, but speakers employed similar ways of talking about the past, even when they hadn't seen each other for decades. This challenged us: How was it that people talked about the same place similarly if they hadn't seen it and each other for so long? How was it that people of different families and distinct ethnicities and individuals with very different life trajectories could relate to each other so effectively after nearly a half-century apart? What exactly was "collective" about their representations, and what were the grounds for this commonality?

These questions have taken us back to the beginning to consider what is "collective" about memory. We have found inspiration in work on distributed cognition and Bruno Latour's actor-network theory (ANT).[51] In his "cognitive ethnography" of ship navigation, Edwin Hutchins advances an understanding of how cognition might be distributed with rich description of teams working together, using tools and other media.[52] Norma Mendoza-Denton builds on these insights in her work with Latina gang members and explores how anonymous artifacts, narrative knowledge, and specific linguistic forms circulate as a form of "distributed memory": "No one person or entity could hold all the pieces to this memory. Every individual had a slightly different collection of personal artifacts."[53]

Such a model of "distributed memory" works well with an ANT approach, for in this model, social groups are not assumed to exist but are perceived as problems to be explained. So too is any other construct modified by the adjective "social." Rather than starting with the assumption of a "social memory" out there, some mystical force connecting members of some "social" group, we instead should ask: If there is some kind of connection between a set of individuals, how did that connection happen? Is it ongoing? How are the linkages maintained? Rather than assuming some mystical "group mind" and then trying to describe its content, we are working in the opposite direction to ask: Which individuals are interested in coming to reunions and why? How and why do they talk about specific pasts, and what does this sharing do? Latour also encourages us to broaden our understanding of actors to think beyond human intentionality. In his view, "any thing that does modify a state of affairs by making a difference is an actor—or, if it has no figuration yet, an actant," adding that the "continuity of any course of action will rarely consist of human-to-human connections . . . or of object-object connections, but will probably zigzag from one to the other."[54] Viewed in this light, reunions themselves become key actants, "instigators," as Jerry put it, motivating people to join together, to assemble. Even the stories they share can be viewed as motivating, as they compel people to reciprocate, swapping stories and thus talking about certain topics in certain ways.

The reunions expose us to shared remembering as it is happening.[55] This book documents the assembling of individuals, their reassembling, really, each with his or her own individual life experiences coming together to recollect a collective past. This collection of individuals does not represent a tight-knit group but rather involves a set of people attached to the same missing place. Because of the mobility of their families in the 1930s through the 1960s, some are old childhood friends who haven't seen each other in years, and others have never met before but had lived on the same street during a different decade. Rather than approaching collective memory as some mysterious shared essence everyone retains, we emphasize the work that people undertake in gathering, a processual activity that is ongoing, that takes effort, that people engage in together. It is for this reason that we say that this book is the study of a "collective remembering," an ongoing activity necessarily interrupted in the telling, for it is ongoing while we write.

The Language of Remembering

A central question in studies of people's relationship to the past is *how* memory is "distributed" both "across individuals" and "between agents and the cultural tools they employ to think, remember, and carry out other forms of action."[56] In our study, language became the most important cultural tool that allowed us to explore the sharing of memories. A rich tradition in linguistic anthropology considers the role of the past in language use, and we build on this work, recognizing language as one of the principal means of consolidating and sharing common understandings: it is a collective mnemonic par excellence.[57]

A study of local language ideologies buttressed by close analysis of language in use often reveals strategic means by which actors bring the past into contemporary politics and social interactions. Miyako Inoue discusses new insights generated from studies of language ideologies as a "historic turn," "a renewed attention to and theorization of the history, historicity, and temporality of language and of linguistic practice as well as linguistic change. The historical dimension has been reinserted into linguistic and semiotic analysis by the insistence that language is part and parcel of the material world, the historically dynamic world, in which real actors live."[58] As Brigittine French puts it in a recent review article, linguistic anthropologists have begun to outline with precision the "semiotic and discursive mechanisms by which the past is selectively brought into the present for strategic ends."[59]

Since we knew we wanted to explore not only the content of our speakers' stories but also the way that they told them, we taped as many of the discussions as possible, even when the excitement and energetic nature of the interactions made for difficult transcription indeed. We also tried to interfere as little as possible to avoid introducing our own periodicity or language into their discussions,[60] first presenting our topic with open-ended statements such as "tell us about life in the old neighborhood." These interviews were extended with insights drawn from two college research methods classes, as we explain below. This study, then, is based on field notes of these meetings and on taped and transcribed one-on-one and group interviews held at individuals' homes or at the reunions. Our interviewees' ages ranged from 60 to 102, with most in their seventies and eighties (born between 1928 and 1936). Most of them graduated high school in the mid-1940s to 1950s and started families in the neighborhood at that time. Those of foreign origins were all born in the United States; many had parents or grandparents born in what is now Lebanon or Italy. We met with an equal number of men and women. They told stories of Syrian Town as it was in the late 1930s to the 1960s; their stories have an exact cut-off point (1964) because the neighborhood was destroyed so abruptly.

The corpus of stories and anecdotes that we have collected do not easily fall into one narrative genre, perhaps because they were told by members of a community that was shattered some fifty years ago. This is not a classic study following a discrete group of people over their everyday activities. Because they do not represent an ongoing community, they have not as a group maintained patterned storytelling practices.[61] Work on historical narrative often explores skilled orality (oracy) and master performances.[62] At the other end of the spectrum are "personal narratives," or "everyday conversational narratives of personal experiences."[63] While largely about the past, our stories include many personal anecdotes, and several of Elinor Ochs and Lisa Capps's observations about "personal narratives" provide a useful way to frame our corpus.

Ochs and Capps emphasize the interactive nature of personal narratives. They distinguish "the teller" (animator, in Erving Goffman's language) from the "author," for even silent participants may be authors. Usually such narratives involve multiple "tellers" who contribute to the evolution of a narrative in a wide range of ways, with high and low levels of involvement; at one extreme are one-on-one formal interviews, which may have relatively low involvement by the "audience" or listener, and at the other are family dinner conversations in which multiple participants may join together in telling a story. As they write, "narratives told in informal conversation often have multiple tellers who ask questions, react, and otherwise contribute what they know, believe, or feel about some life incident." Even listeners can become authors or narrators, and tellers can "coax" others into speaking by asking for their reaction to the story they are telling.[64] Our data thus fall on the extreme end of coconstructed testimonials: because our methodology included recordings and observations of multiple people interacting together as they talked about the past, sometimes during simultaneously recorded sessions in the same room, they not only constructed their stories together but often called out to members of other groups for assistance when they couldn't remember the name of a person or place. We were often brought in through a discussion about the terms or topics under way in part to help the student narrators understand the points being made.

Carrying this insight from Ochs and Capps one step further, we pursued the collisions, the clashes, the disjunctures between Syrian Towners' ways of seeing the world and ours. In their article on the return of ethnographic theory, Giovanni da Col and David Graeber describe ethnography as "pragmatic inquiry into *conceptual disjunctures*."[65] To engage the disjunctures we encountered about the Syrian Town of yesteryear required that we attend to the local specificity in the work of language. We explore how narratives about Syrian Town employ words and phrases that were used in the old neighborhood but are now outdated. Using these "past terms" conjures up images of the area before demolition; by virtue of their deep association with Syrian Town life, the terms are imbued with productive energy that helps trigger further remembering. In this way, the linguistic items themselves serve as "actants," in Latour's sense, or as "instigators," to use Jerry's term.

The "tellability" of personal narratives is another point Ochs and Capps underscore. They argue that narratives can have different degrees of interest,[66] and they discuss how children are socialized to know what is tellable and what is not. We would like to emphasize the *contextual* nature of "tellability": we heard many stories that were only tellable in this particular context due to the copresence of other individuals who knew about the places and situations mentioned (e.g., stories about a now-gone movie theater would have little meaning to contemporary Eastonians). The reuniting of former friends and neighbors seemed to unleash these stories, and the stories themselves shifted from untellable to tellable. As one man said energetically to his wife, "It's nice to have this [reunion]. Because you know, you tell these stories to people who didn't grow up in Easton and you begin to wonder if maybe you're exaggerating what is was like to live in Easton. So it's nice to hear affirmation. As we've been sitting here listening to other people, I'm saying to my wife, 'See?! See?!'" We may have unwittingly played a role in this shift from untellable to tellable, for our very presence and research interests signaled people's childhood memories as worthy of scholarly attention, validating them as worth telling and even recording.

The contextual nature of tellability becomes clear too when we situate these narratives within the contemporary racial order, which reveals the fundamentally political nature of these recollections. This leads us finally to "moral stance." Ochs and Capps write that personal narratives "elaborately encode and perpetuate moral world views," and the everyday narration of life experience is a "primary medium for moral education."[67] We will discuss how the stories of Syrian Town contained a similar moral stance that was overtly and covertly contrasted to the contemporary world order.

"Here Are the Instigators!"

In describing the gatherings that made possible the Syrian Town storytelling, we are sensitive to the multiple and easily overlooked "actors," both human and nonhuman.[68] We, as researchers and authors, certainly count as well. As Jerry once announced, calling us "instigators," we are partly responsible for the very remembering that we are analyzing. Here, we pause to consider our own positions as researchers approaching this project.

The ethnographic enterprise requires a unique kind of total commitment and full immersion that is difficult to maintain from afar. In some ways, this project offered relief from the lingering guilt one feels when leaving one's research community at the end of a summer research stint, as dictated by the academic calendar. But carrying out an ongoing project while teaching or studying in the same town carries its own challenges. Phone calls from community members ramped up before and after each reunion we held as people thought of new people to invite or informed us of a recent move, illness, or new address. Andrea often held impromptu interviews with elderly men and women who had additional points to make about a former time and place—and these calls invariably occurred right before class or when a student was in Andrea's office. Our field notes include a great number of handwritten jottings hastily recorded on the fly. Working with the very old poses additional challenges: we have been invited to more funerals than we can attend, and it is uncomfortable forgoing the funeral of a close friend and informant in order to give a lecture or attend a faculty meeting.

Andrea was Anna's college professor. She began teaching and mentoring Anna at the very beginning of Anna's undergraduate career, and they pursued this project together during summers, between classes, and through late-night emails throughout the course of Anna's time in college. Lafayette College's generous undergraduate research funding structure facilitated her involvement, with the structure of the funding program itself serving as another sort of "instigator": since funding was easily renewed, it provided an open-endedness that encouraged Anna and Andrea to explore Syrian Town in the underdetermined format that is so central to ethnography. This kind of financial support, rarely available for undergraduates, was instrumental in allowing Anna to remain on the campus during the summers and thereby to be present *in* the spaces where the reunions, conversations, and remembering were happening.

If we are "instigators," then we like to think of our role as encouraging the rememberers of Syrian Town. Our support was at once political and pragmatic. We often felt they read our presence as a mark of legitimacy finally granted to a group so long silenced by official narratives. And in practical terms, we provided labor and basic material support. As "instigators," we helped by developing an active database of former residents, which we reconstructed from *Polk's Easton City Directory* the year before demolition started (1963), updating it by seeking former residents' current addresses. We scheduled a room in which to meet and sent out announcement flyers. The flyers themselves can be seen as "instigators," for they helped to organize everyone into the same place at the same time. (Their vital role became evident when they did not reach their intended audience, causing some people to miss a meeting and call us afterward to complain.) And as we describe these gatherings, the number of such "actors" multiplies; as participants in them, we too were swept along by the momentum as the research proceeded.

A Place for Remembering: Events as Instigators

Our project gained real traction after a remarkable elementary school reunion held by a local church in 2008, which drew far more local interest than even the organizers imagined possible. People were so thrilled to get together with others from the old neighborhood and reminisce that they immediately began organizing subsequent get-togethers. We had planned to carry out a series of interviews with former neighbors but soon learned that our interviewees were most interested in meeting with each other ("like the other Taylor School reunion," they explained), and we helped plan these events, holding them at the same location. Our project then became partly collaborative anthropology as we adjusted our research design to accommodate the participants' desire for more reunions.[69]

We also held large focus-group-type discussions during a Father's Day dinner hosted by the local Maronite Church; at "scan-a-thons" held at both the Lutheran and Lebanese churches, during which students helped scan old images of the neighborhood; and at an unofficial neighborhood reunion held weekly at a local bar. We taped or took notes during conversations at these events and followed up with taped private interviews at the public library and in private homes.

We held most of the large events at St. John's Lutheran Church, site of the 2008 reunion and one of the few neighborhood structures that had not been demolished. For most reunion events, then, people were actually returning to one of the last surviving neighborhood structures. We called these Taylor School Reunions, referencing the elementary school that had been next door to the church. The church has an easily accessible parking lot, which is one of the reasons we chose it as our venue, but, interestingly enough, the parking lot is exactly where the Taylor School used to stand. Because of this, Taylor School alumni who otherwise would not have been comfortable going into the church of another denomination could overlook this barrier. We might see the school, the church, or even the parking lot itself as actors, and when we tried to hold events at other locations, attendance was paltry. Moreover, any other location could not attract a turnout that actually mirrored the school's (and neighborhood's) ethnic makeup. The parking lot, formed because the school was torn down, created the only place where we could hold a successful meeting for this group.

At the reunions, former residents were eager to talk with one another, and there was a buzz of excitement in the air. Not knowing what to expect

FIG. 3. Meeting in the church basement. Image courtesy of Andrea Smith.

during our first two reunions, we brought visual aids to help start conversations, including some old photographs, historical Sanborn Company fire insurance maps of the demolished neighborhood featuring detailed views of each structure, and photocopied pages from the directory. The response to these items was overwhelmingly enthusiastic. People *loved* reading through the directory pages and reminiscing about the locations of the neighborhood's different stores and homes. Interestingly, we had begun our research about the neighborhood with these items, for they helped us reconstruct that part of the city before its demolition and track down remaining former residents. To us, these items were clues to a lost world. To our interviewees (whom we had to search for, given that our knowledge of them came from archival records), the items validated the memories that they held, archived in their minds as artifacts of a bygone era.

As interest continued to grow, we involved a college class in 2014 and 2015. This again was partly community inspired. Motivated by the success of the reunions, they asked the lead author if she might prepare a book of neighborhood memories that they could share with the next generation. Seeing this as an opportunity to also train students in ethnographic research methods, Andrea created a new course that involved additional students who participated in reunions, taped interviews, and prepared a student-authored book of memories that will likely become an actor in and of itself.[70] Fieldwork since 2007 was thus complemented by two semesters of working with student and elderly resident teams as they navigated recollecting together. These interactions sometimes led to unique observations or interesting confusions related to the wide age gap between the speakers, as we address later in this book.

Fieldwork Dialectics: Instigating the Instigators

While we certainly played a role in facilitating the recollecting we describe in this book, we in turn were motivated—reinvigorated even—by people who had already taken it upon themselves to piece together vestiges of their shattered world. When Andrea conducted research with French settlers of Algeria, she once encountered a man who had created a whole social club involving former residents of his hometown, Mondovi. He started with a mental map of the village and began listing people house by house. He then began looking for these names on the Minitel, the French national telephone directory, a precursor to the Internet. After years of work in this way, he had located enough people across France to hold a reunion.[71] A similar drive motivates some of the people we present here. Mark, for instance, is an African American man in his mideighties who spent his working life in dry cleaning. He provided us with the majority of the current addresses of the former residents we met. We had insight into his unique character when one day a birthday card arrived in Andrea's mailbox. When she called Mark to thank him, he announced, "You're on the list!" It was at that point that we learned that he is a self-designated "keeper of addresses" who sends out over two hundred birthday cards a year, mostly to former residents of Syrian Town. "It's my thing," he explained simply.

Like the birthday cards, the reunions we helped plan served as venues for recollecting Syrian Town, for "reassembling the social."[72] There were other venues too that we did not help create: certain graduating classes of Easton High School get together once monthly for brunch, and there is the weekly neighborhood reunion held at a local bar that Eddie had "discovered." Additionally, Our Lady of Lebanon Church holds an annual Lebanese festival in the town at its new location. Since the majority of the local Lebanese population had lived in the area that was demolished, these events sometimes attract people of other ethnic backgrounds as well who want to see, support, and reminisce with their old Lebanese neighbors. Through these practices, people engage in the active production of both memory and identity.

We also learned of some individuals' efforts to preserve the memory of Syrian Town through material culture. Jerry told us he offers walking tours. Despite his cane, he takes people around the city, pointing out where certain old buildings had stood and telling people about life in the old neighborhood. He teaches them how to read the city's sidewalks and building materials as a guide to which sections had been built when. He doesn't want people to take the city's history for granted.

Another man, Larry, serves as a self-appointed curator of Easton's past. Following the first reunion, this well-spoken retired gentleman invited us to his suburban home to see his "Easton collection." We went down to the unfinished basement and into a room with floor-to-ceiling shelves along its perimeter that were stuffed absolutely full of books, photographs, road signs, jerseys, trophies, and trinkets. The middle of the room was taken up by stacks of papers and more paraphernalia, two chairs, and Larry's desk, which had an old computer on it. He took a seat at his desk and told us about some of the contents of this archive. Most of the items were not his own but had been given to him by others who heard about his collection. Larry showed us several PowerPoint slide shows of photographs of the city before demolition. In one, he featured the area's schools; another showed images taken during various floods. He painstakingly explained the content of each image: what each building was called, what went on there, and who owned it. Larry told us he visits local schools to teach young people about Easton's history, showing them these presentation slides. He also produces an "Easton Remembered" calendar annually, featuring a different old photograph each month. In addition to selling the calendars locally, he distributes them to old friends, mailing them off to those whose contact information he still has. His enduring contact with old neighbors emanated from the exchange of neighborhood goods: they give or send him relics of bygone days such as photos and memorabilia, and he turns them into forms that

FIG. 4. Resident brings photograph to reunion. Image courtesy of Luis Gomez.

can circulate more widely to former residents and anyone interested in the city's past. And an even more recent example is a Facebook page, *You Know You're from Easton* . . . , which has been a remarkable source of old photographs of the town in yesteryear and boasts nearly six thousand members.

In these cases, individuals physically separated have taken it upon themselves to reassemble former elements of Syrian Town and ensure that they are preserved, their significance recognized. An elderly, physically handicapped man continues to dedicate himself to passing on the stories of the past in addition to the markers that corroborate them. A retired man uses a large portion of his basement and a large portion of his time to store and circulate objects and images that can now index a place to which no one can ever go back.

The process of conducting research, then, was part of a process that was already under way. In some ways, our experience bears a similarity to Joëlle Bahloul's research with families who remembered living in a household in colonial Algeria. She writes that her ethnographic initiative "did not create but awakened" the process of remembering. As people came together, they sought to affirm their connection to their past, "a past represented in human form by their former neighbors who had reappeared in their lives like a surrealistic vision with my impromptu visit."[73] Similarly, we found ourselves with people who were coming together often for the first time since the demolitions; or, rather, they found themselves with us. Our project and presence helped facilitate their remembering of the collective past *together*: not as individuals isolated from one another but as a social enterprise. The persons, photos, and items they encountered at the reunions served as mnemonic devices for what life had been in the past. Specific linguistic practices, too, play a significant role in evoking the Syrian Town of the past. As we will show, new words and ways of speaking do not erase the previous ways of thinking/speaking; people have access to the former ways of speaking that make up their whole language biography.[74] The language that developed as people engaged with and were engaged upon by past places is never systematically erased, and as a result, the affective power of lost places can interrupt everyday life in the present through narration.

The special context of our interviews—discussions of a world that vanished almost overnight—provided an unusual point from which to hear our interviewees' narratives. Scholars of social memory regularly acknowledge that accounts of the past are necessarily colored by present-day considerations.[75] We will consider the ways stories of Syrian Town take on a new urgency given the segregated nature of the contemporary cityscape. These ways of engaging in nostalgic trips to a former place in time can be viewed as subversive and even as creative place building, the focus of the concluding chapter. Leading up to that, the book as a whole engages the ways that Syrian Town is remembered. In chapter 2, we unpack the destruction of Syrian Town and the process by which the area was labeled "blighted." Chapter 3 examines how former Syrian Town residents discuss difference, paying close attention to the local vernacular and its mixing of distinctions more typically viewed as markers of race, ethnicity, nationality, or class and their relationship to place. Chapter 4 interrogates the outdated styles of speaking to which narrators reverted when they talked about the old neighborhood, foregrounding the use of "temporal heteroglossia" in their speech. Chapter 5 explores how those specific narration practices described in the previous two chapters work in concert with other material forces to call up the images, relationships, and modes of sociality that defined life in Syrian Town while it was still standing. Finally, chapter 6 considers the everyday political significance of recollecting Syrian Town, a practice in which former residents are deeply invested.

2. The Language of Blight

When we met Francine at a local bar in 2007, it seemed that the destruction of her former neighborhood had just occurred. She was ten when she was forced out. "February," she said while sipping a beer at the bar run by Sami, a former neighbor also of Lebanese descent. "February 1963. We fought it and fought it," she added. "We told them we'd do whatever it took to improve the houses." ("But no, they weren't interested in that," her male companion interjected.) Francine spoke of that terrible time: "I remember standing across the street and watching them take down our house." Francine and her friend Ellen were in their mid-sixties. Both had cropped dark hair. They were sitting at the old wooden bar eating hamburgers and fries. Francine added, "Those houses were stripped." She remembered how people came and took out all the sinks and other fixtures before they were demolished. She went on to describe her former home in detail: the balcony she and her sister had off their bedroom, the yard, the two-car garage. "Progress, redevelopment," she quipped with some sarcasm. "They tried to tell us we were in a blighted area, but it wasn't. What's blighted now is downtown Easton!"

Many people we met seemed stunned by the dramatic change to the cityscape and still had difficulty comprehending what had happened, even though it had occurred a half-century before. The urban renewal that they experienced was so sudden and so complete that they continue to talk about it with a mixture of confusion and disbelief. Susan, a woman of Italian descent, met us in her home and brought out photocopied images of some of the vanished streets. While showing us a picture of the Northampton Street Bridge with homes in the background, she added, "You can see here the amount of homes they tore down. I don't know why they did that." Mrs. Godfrey's assessment that project backers were "radicals" was shared by Susan's husband, Joseph, a retired high school teacher with a shock of white hair. He described the process as "fevered": "They waved their hands and it was gone." He felt that the area had not been in bad shape at all: "Some houses in the back alleys may not have been perfect, but even those were nice. But they just mowed them down." The philosophy of the time contrasted with today's "spot redevelopment," he explained. "In those days, if you had one bad house, you took out the whole block," adding, "Once you start leveling, where do you draw the line?"

Blighted structures or sound ones? Site of decay or thriving neighborhood? Justified demolition or not? During our first years of interviews, it sometimes felt as if we were listening to testimony in an extended hearing, with us positioned as judge and jury as our interviewees challenged the rationale officials used for the urban renewal projects that had attacked their neighborhood. We also heard extensive descriptions of demolished structures: how solid the foundation, what kinds of flooring the residents had installed, the cost of the mantelpiece over the fireplace. We heard who was responsible, what mistakes were made, who benefited. In this chapter, we look at the rise and fall of Syrian Town, highlighting the varying ways people understand the renewal process that altered the face of the city and set their lives on new tracks altogether. "Blight," we found, is a pivotal trope in these narratives, a multivalent term that is used by city officials to defend their actions and that is directly challenged by former residents. We will consider reasons for selecting this part of the city specifically, asking whether it was the Lebanese character of the neighborhood that drew the attention of city leaders, race, its ethnic mixture, or other factors altogether. But first, we provide a richer description of Syrian Town on the eve of its demolition.

Making Syrian Town

Journalist Eileen Kenna depicted Syrian Town on the eve of its demolition as follows:

It's a muggy summer evening. . . . A group of men sit drinking Turkish coffee and talking "old country" politics in the smoke-filled Karam's Café at Lehigh and Bank streets. Outdoors on South Fourth and Lehigh

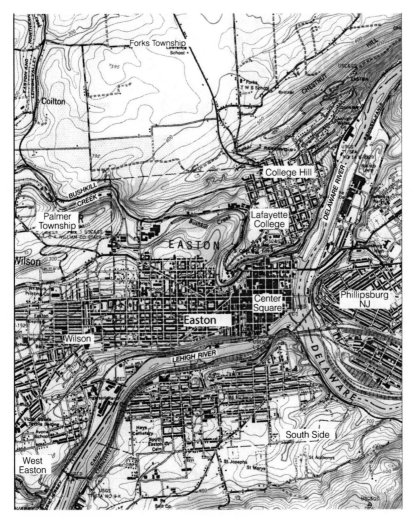

MAP 1. Easton, Pennsylvania, and surrounding area. Source: 1953 U.S. Geographical Survey topographical map. Adapted by Kristin Leader.

streets, a few white-haired women in black dresses and black stockings sit on sagging front stoops, gazing at the shouting children who dart among the dusky shadows on the street. . . . Nearby, adults and kids savor refreshing, homemade lemon ice from Thomas' corner grocery store at the bottom of the Lehigh Street hill. On most warm days like this one, South Fourth and roughly a three block radius surrounding it pulsate with the sounds of voices speaking English and Arabic—often a lively combination of the two—while aromas of garlic and baking bread lace the air.[1]

This neighborhood was located in downtown Easton, Pennsylvania, quite close to the confluence of the Delaware and Lehigh Rivers.[2] When Easton was established in 1752 as the Northampton County seat, the county was predominantly agricultural and remained so until industrial growth ramped up in the mid-nineteenth century. German-speaking settlers outnumbered all others at first; the first English-language paper was published there in 1799.[3] The city became more ethnically diverse with industrialization. By the turn of the twentieth century it was a bustling industrial, transportation, and commercial hub. Canals bordering both rivers were used to ship coal from the coalfields northwest of the city, and railroad lines connected the city to Allentown and Bethlehem to the west, New York City to the east, and Philadelphia to the south.

Easton's "Syrians" began arriving in the area in 1900. They were Maronite Catholics, almost exclusively from the same village (Kfarsghab). The neighborhood they settled in had experienced regular ethnic succession. Early German stock was joined by immigrants from Wales, Ireland, and England in the early 1800s.[4] The Irish Catholic population soon grew large enough to support St. Bernard's Parish, formed in 1829. Easton's Jewish community, one of the oldest in the country, established a synagogue on nearby streets in 1839. Blacks were living in this part of Easton quite early on as well, forming the First Colored Evangelical Lutheran Church of Easton in 1866, affiliated with the current St. John's Evangelical Lutheran Church, where we held the reunions.[5] Migrants fleeing Russian Empire pogroms formed a second Jewish congregation on Spruce Street in 1889. Southern Italians arrived after the turn of the century and established their own congregation in 1916; they were attracted by opportunities in local quarries, construction, the Bethlehem Steel plant, and local silk mills.[6]

This was a crowded part of town composed of two- and three-story frame and brick row houses. To the south was the main passenger train station, where our speakers would sometimes play as children; freight depots; and industrial facilities along the Lehigh River, including grocery

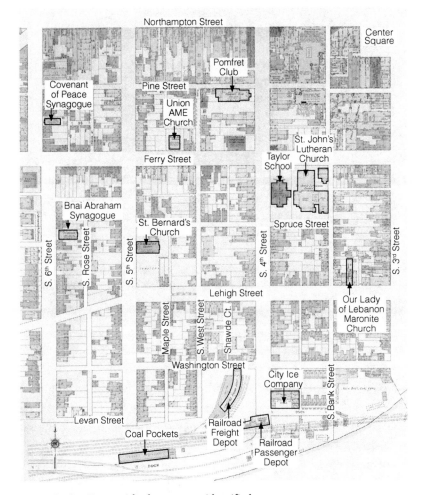

MAP 2. Syrian Town with place-names identified.

warehouses, coal yard storage, and the ice company's storehouses and stables. At its north end was the city's central shopping district, Center Square. Some residents ran boardinghouses for men who worked in local or nearby foundries, textile and steel mills, and other industries. This was a working-class community, and many of the people we interviewed had friends who went to work in factories rather than finishing high school.

Independent shops lined the streets: we heard of family-run groceries, bakeries, butchers, pharmacies, and cobblers. Many of Easton's Leb-

E-4   BIRD'S-EYE VIEW OF BUSINESS SECTION, EASTON, PA.

7-H835

FIG. 5. *Bird's-Eye View of Business Section, Easton* PA. Color linen-texture printed postcard published by Lynn H. Boyer, Philadelphia PA and Wildwood NJ, postmarked 1938. This view of Easton is from across the Lehigh River, ca. 1930. Located at the intersection of two rivers, the city grew, attracting businesses and canal and rail traffic. In the foreground are the city's large passenger station and the passenger and freight lines of the Central Railroad of New Jersey.

anese started as peddlers, brought to Easton at the request of a New York supplier.[7] Our interviewees remembered their relatives walking miles from Easton's center to sell notions to farmers in the surrounding townships. The ideal peddler career trajectory involved slow but steady savings, leading to the purchase of a wagon and, ultimately, an independent dry goods store.[8] By the 1920s this transition was already under way in Easton: more Lebanese by this time owned shops than peddled, and the remainder worked in local factories.[9] Lebanese households by this time often contained extended families and included second-generation Pennsylvania-born children along with additional relatives, such as the household heads' parents, siblings, or cousins. This growing population of "Assyrians" raised some local alarm; in 1916 journalists reported about the "rioting" of "warring Assyrians" on Lehigh and South Bank Streets and suggested that even the police were nervous.[10]

By the 1930s many Italian and Lebanese immigrant families had transitioned from being tenants to homeowners.[11] After World War II many families of Russian Jewish, Italian, and Pennsylvania German descent left for the surrounding suburbs and the city's more exclusive neighborhoods, such as College Hill, while more blacks were moving in. While some long-standing black families owned their homes on neighborhood streets as early as 1930, other blacks arrived to the neighborhood from southern states and worked for the railroad and in the steel mills or as private drivers, maids, and chefs.[12] Yet the black population in the overall city remained minuscule and composed only 1 percent of the city's population in 1950.

Our speakers emphasized the liveliness of the streets and the rich texture of urban life, a texture determined in large part by the close interpenetration of residences and industry. People worked and lived in the downtown area. Because people worked different hours, someone was always on the street getting ready for work or coming home. "The streets were always alive," one woman explained. She said that she would return home from work at a nearby Lebanese tavern at two o'clock in the morning to find older men still on the stoops talking. Lights would soon shine from the home of the local baker.

This liveliness was sometimes too much. Dorothy, a woman of Lebanese descent in her seventies, talked about staying over at the house of a friend whose mother ran a bar: "I couldn't sleep there, there was so much noise. Friday night, people come into the bar. I slept over one night, and I said never again!" But in some ways, her grandmother's chickens got their revenge. One day, the owner of the same bar had enough: "You know, five o'clock comes, the chickens start yelling away, it's morning. My friend's mother, she comes down, and she's yelling at my grandfather: 'You know, those damns chickens don't let us sleep!' He's like, 'I'm sorry.' She said, 'Well, you better do something about it.' He says to her, 'Well, you do something about the noisy people coming out of the bar, and I'll do something about the chickens!'"

When we asked former residents to describe life in the neighborhood, they often exclaimed, "We never used to lock our doors!" One woman told us that her aunt did not even own a key until renewal forced her out of her home. This frequent refrain indicated a sense of safety and familiarity with one's neighbors and implicitly contrasted practices found in the same area today. In the old neighborhood, the interviewees told

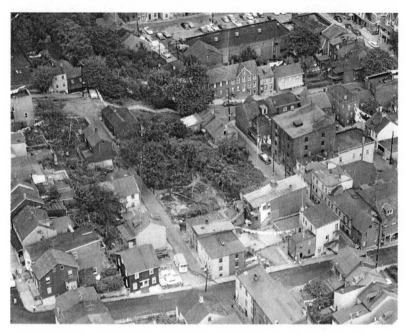

FIG. 6. Aerial view of 5th Street before redevelopment. Image courtesy of Len Buscemi.

us, people used to look after each other. We heard this from interviewees of all backgrounds. A black woman described it as a "real" neighborhood where "you were everybody's child." So what happened, and how did it all end?

"Redevelopment Ruined Easton"

People today discuss the demolitions that targeted Syrian Town in terms that suggest a murky notion of the process at work. When asked how the decision was made to demolish his store, one eighty-eight-year-old grocer, Oliver, said simply, "Redevelopment came, and they didn't care about you." "Redevelopment" simply arrived in Easton. When asked who was in charge of urban renewal, another man replied, "I don't know who it was—I'm sure it had to come out of Washington, then it trickled down into the locals. They used to call it Easton Redevelopment Authority, they had to do what they had to do because, you know, it was probably their job. It just happened, that's all." Sometimes people talked about "the City" as the principal actor. A Lebanese woman in her late seventies explained, "The City—the City had the say-so."

For many, "redevelopment" was a villain. One woman told us, "Once the redevelopment came, it broke up the community." Her friend concurred. She discussed life in the former neighborhood in rosy terms, concluding, "Until the redevelopment came to improve Easton." In most cases, people used the word "redevelopment" to refer to a general process, but sometimes it was unclear if they were also referring to the responsible local agency, the Easton Redevelopment Authority (ERA). Agatha stated outright in the first minutes of our conversation, "Now, who ruined Easton? You could put it in [your] paper: redevelopment ruined Easton!" These statements suggest a real alienation from local government and the political process. Redevelopment appears akin to a force of nature that arrived and then left, a process into which residents had little input or influence.

Other interviewees saw redevelopment in Easton as only a microcosm of larger urban renewal efforts around the country. The realization that redevelopment was happening nationwide allowed our interviewees to feel that they were not suffering alone. Sami's wife, Josie, asked Francine and Ellen, "Didn't the same thing happen in Scranton?" That similar renewal processes occurred just seventy miles northeast of Easton illustrated the prevalence and extensiveness of redevelopment. Oliver told us, "Redevelopment was happening all over. The same thing happened to my mother's two sisters in Providence" (Rhode Island).

Some people blame specific individuals to this day. Francine was quite clear about who destroyed her neighborhood. "Mayor George Smith!" she shouted out to us between bites of hamburger. "They gave my parents $5,300 for their house," she added. "They were the first to go." Former schoolteacher Joseph also mentioned Mayor Smith and added, laughing, "They named a bridge after the man who destroyed our city." Yet Smith, mayor when the project was conceived and carried out, was not the only person impugned. Other interviewees blamed members of the Easton Redevelopment Authority who they felt must have made money on the side. And yet no clear consensus emerged regarding who was behind the project and stood to gain from it. Thus, like people who discussed the experience in vague terms, those who identified specific villains also were puzzled by the whole process. When we asked Joseph who had benefited from redevelopment, he replied, "Who knows?! I wish I could tell you." He suggested that perhaps the owner of a small gas station benefited, adding, "Someone benefited, you know someone did. Money went into someone's pocket, I'm sure."

While they apparently did not know exactly who was running the renewal project, former residents did have a clear sense of the rationale city officials had given for it. These authorities, many said, thought their neighborhood was a great source of "blight," an assessment they passionately contested. As Francine told us, "They said that the area was 'blighted,' but it really wasn't. In the eyes of the mayor, the area was 'blighted.'" Susan also stated emphatically, "Most of the homes they tore down were brick. Politicians at the time would tell you that they were crap, but they really weren't." Ellen explained, "They said that our houses were slums. Our houses were not slums. Hardwood floors? Every house had hardwood floors, oak, mahogany." Former homeowners consistently defended the quality of their properties, often giving elaborate descriptions of their homes that had been razed. Agatha, for instance, told us, "I had a finished-off cellar, I had a beautiful cellar, I had it all done over like an apartment. And my first floor, I had all hardwood floors. [We excerpt discussions of repairs.] I had paneling in every room. I had put—I wish I could have found the pictures! My daughter lost a bag of pictures. I had a *beautiful* picture window. My home was . . . repaired and brought *past* up to date. It was beautiful."

Another man contrasted the homes they were encouraged to move into with the quality of homes the city wanted to tear down: "They wanted us to move, they said, 'How about if we move you to Wilson Borough?' Between 15th and 16th Streets there were townhouses, very small, one, two, three bedrooms—they wanted us to move there. The home we used to live in [he states his address here], where the windows were, they had marble. We had solid oak steps going up, three stories plus a full basement. They were built with double brick—they were fantastic buildings." In his view, city officials labeled the homes as blighted so that they could tear them down. "That's how they labeled them to rip them down, you know, by eminent domain."

"A Sensible Reuse Pattern"

Syrian Town was eradicated in stages by a series of renewal projects. The first, the Lehigh-Washington Street project, targeted Syrian Town's very heart and is our focus here. Described as "one of the most drawn out and difficult urban renewal projects in the Lehigh Valley," this was the fourth redevelopment project undertaken by city officials, who were facing postwar deindustrialization and the development of the rural areas ringing the city.[13] What drew city leaders to this lively part of town?

Easton had been the region's premier shopping center, but by the 1950s it was losing its allure to suburban malls, and its population was declining. A county planning commission report on the Central Business District (CBD) noted, "The population of Easton declined by over 3,000 people between 1950 and 1960," representing a nearly 10 percent population loss. The report went on to argue that population decline was not the entire story. Instead, Easton's share of consumer spending was "declining absolutely and relatively." Even though retail sales in the CBD continued to increase between 1954 and 1958, city leaders were worried because this increase was dwarfed by growth in the surrounding areas. Analysts argued that downtown businesses could not present an "atmosphere conducive to attracting shoppers." They described building conditions as "generally poor" and parking as inadequate, and they lamented that the "mixed utilization of land fail[ed] to create an aesthetic appearance." The report noted the real risk of further erosion of the CBD, the city's most important tax base sector.[14] Reports such as this one convinced city officials that they needed to revitalize the commercial portion of downtown Easton to draw suburbanites back to the city's shopping district.

The timing of a natural disaster (1955) proved fortuitous for development interests. In the wake of flooding caused by Hurricane Diane, the City Planning Commission "seized the opportunity" to qualify 197 city acres along the Lehigh and Delaware Rivers for redevelopment under the Federal Urban Renewal Program.[15] As the consultants developing the city's 1957 Comprehensive Plan noted, the area, known as the Diane Flood Project, "will permit replanning of a substantial portion of the downtown area of Easton."[16] Despite the fact that there was "no discernible loss of the historic structures that lined the waterfront," as Timothy

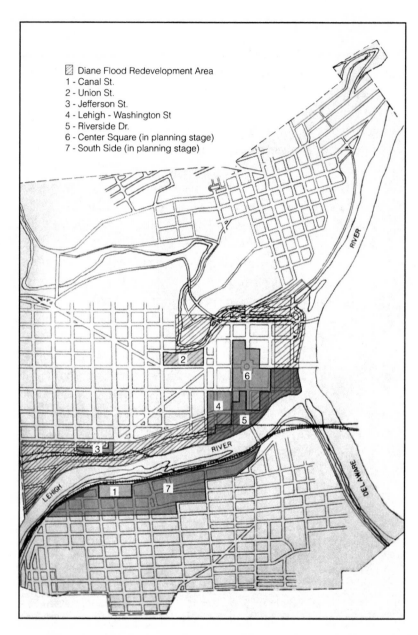

Diane Flood Redevelopment Area
1 - Canal St.
2 - Union St.
3 - Jefferson St.
4 - Lehigh - Washington St
5 - Riverside Dr.
6 - Center Square (in planning stage)
7 - South Side (in planning stage)

MAP 3. Easton's urban renewal projects, ca. 1967. Source: "A Report on the Comprehensive General Plan of the City of Easton, PA—1957," unpublished report by the Easton City Planning Commission, 21. Courtesy of the city of Easton PA. Adapted by Kristin Leader.

Hare has written, the city's renewal efforts after the flood left an "unprecedented wake of architectural destruction."[17] The Easton Redevelopment Authority commenced its first project, the Canal Street project, one year after the hurricane. This project involved the demolition of forty-eight homes on the south side of the Lehigh River and preparation of the land for industrial use. Luring developers proved more difficult than planners had anticipated, however. The land was still vacant in 1963, and two years later the project was referred to as "the Canal Street fiasco."[18] Two smaller projects, the Union Street and Jefferson Street renewal projects, followed. City officials later considered these projects more successful because the cleared lands were rebuilt with homes for low-rent and low-income public housing, nearly replacing the demolished housing units (112 new public housing units replaced 133 demolished units). But they too had their critics.[19]

Formal consideration of the Lehigh-Washington Street area began in the last three months of 1960, although when some of our interviewees first learned about it, there seemed to already be a clearly formulated plan in place. Officials intended the initial venture to involve thirty-eight acres and to be a "joint redevelopment and rehabilitation project" with the city's housing authority, which would purchase some of the land to build high-rise housing for the elderly. City officials pursued the plan energetically. By the end of 1960 an inspection team was half finished, with a "comprehensive substandard survey of every dwelling unit" in the "area bounded by 4th Street, 5th Street, Ferry Street, and the New Jersey Central Railroad," the area that was eventually razed.[20] In January 1961 the City Planning Commission gave preliminary certification for a "Lehigh-Washington Street Urban Renewal area."[21]

Plans advanced rapidly: on November 30, 1962, the federal government approved a planning grant, and a mere month later, the Easton Redevelopment Authority reported that it had completed "forty-five percent of the planning activities." A few weeks after that, the authority requested federal permission to initiate execution, or "acquisition, relocation and demolition."[22] It was on January 24, 1963, that the Easton City Council and City Planning Commission first received a copy of the plan, which had been prepared by Murray-Walker Associates, Inc., a private Philadelphia-based urban planning consulting firm hired by the

Easton Redevelopment Authority. It is no wonder that some city officials expressed surprise, as the plan involved the demolition of the area's 155 structures, including all of its residential ones. At that meeting, John Beiswanger, chair of the City Planning Commission, and commission member John Oldt questioned such an extensive clearing of properties. Joseph Dowell, coordinator of ERA, responded with the city planning philosophy then in vogue: complete clearance was necessary to promote "a sensible reuse pattern" and increase the site's attractiveness to potential developers. It appears that the planners hoped to minimize public response to the project. Murray-Walker representative Michael Lonergan announced that just one public hearing would be held for the entire tract and that in the "consent area," "acquisition of properties" would be speeded up roughly a year.[23]

The outcry was immediate when these plans were made public. Protesters first targeted the proposed demolition of one building in particular: the headquarters of the Northampton County Historical and Genealogical Society, located at the intersection of 4th and Ferry Streets (see figure 1).[24] A thirteen-person delegation met with the Easton City Council a few days after the plans were revealed. Edward Schaible, president of the Historical and Genealogical Society, argued that the building was built in 1833 and provided a good example of the "late federal period style."[25] A letter-writing campaign followed, with writers focusing on the soundness of the structure and the difficulty the historical society would face if forced to find a new location for its museum. After what the *Easton Express* described as a "veritable flood of letters to the editor" from "young and old," "architects and engineers, political scientists, historians, business people and plain lay citizens" against the demolition of a "priceless community asset," the redevelopment authority altered the plan in order to spare the building.[26] As an editorial explained, there was a tension between "redevelopment as an imperative to economic regeneration" and "a proper desire to preserve the rich historical assets that are found only in the older communities."[27]

Somewhat lost in the fray, however, were protests regarding the other 150 structures slated for the wrecking ball. Mrs. Margaret Hagerty, Syrian Town resident of South 4th Street and a member of the Citizens Advisory Committee on the Workable Program, a citizens' action group, met with the city council along with the Historical and Genealogical Society protesters and argued that "all houses in the project area along 4th Street between Ferry and Spruce should be retained, as all but one are of brick construction, and, although old, are in good condition." She called removing them a "wanton waste," and added that the houses shouldn't be demolished "just because we have someone who wants to do some fancy planning in Easton."[28]

Hagerty was not alone. Lebanese residents organized with Father Norman Peters of Our Lady of Lebanon Church at the helm. His protest group, the Lehigh-Washington Citizens Home Preservation Committee, hired a local law firm for assistance, and together they spent much of the next year trying to block the project. They too built their argument around challenging the "blight" claims and pressed city leaders to explain how they came up with the data used to justify demolition.[29]

There was only one public meeting to answer these concerns. Held May 28, 1963, it attracted hundreds of people, and the sentiment at the meeting was largely in opposition to development. Hagerty presented a petition against the project that was signed by 386 people from across the city. Individuals spoke up to defend the quality of their homes. Mrs. Gloria Robinson, an African American woman living at 114 South 5th Street, urged council members to retain houses on her street. She added that she had invested a great deal into her home, "and at 64 I don't think I could start all over again." Rose Salvero, also of South 5th Street, made a similar plea, and a representative of Easton's National Association for the Advancement of Colored People (NAACP) said that a statement on discrimination in Easton's public housing was forthcoming.[30]

Peters's Lehigh-Washington Citizens Home Preservation Committee represented the largest opposition bloc, and he submitted a petition with over five hundred signatures. He also presented an alternative proposal that allowed preservation of "the standard solid structures" along 4th Street, the south side of Ferry Street, on Lehigh Street, and on Washington Street from 4th to West Streets. He argued that these houses were "clean, safe, and sanitary, mostly owner-occupied." He added that all that was needed to preserve them was to "move your program back 100 feet." When asked what the project would do to the Lebanese parish he served, he responded, "It would destroy it." Attorney Coffin, hired by Peters's committee, pressed the city council and Murray-Walker employee Michael Lonergan for the data they were using to justify such widespread demolition. Lonergan replied that "he did not have data on the study with him," but he did concede that some of the buildings were "in good condition."[31]

The local press was largely in favor of development. Although it initially expressed some trepidation, particularly regarding the demolition of the county historical society headquarters, and in February had published an editorial regarding the potential displacement of the city's black population, the *Easton Express* subsequently began publishing a series of prodevelopment editorials, especially in the days leading to the important city council meetings held in May and June.[32] Guest editorials were penned by Joseph Dowell, ERA coordinator, followed by articles by the paper's own editorial board ("Decline of Cities—Heavy Price of Progress," "Third of Easton's Housing Units Unfit," "D-Day for Easton's Renewal," "Can Council Face Renewal Challenge?," "Why City Renewal in L-W Sector?," "Attacks on Renewal Neglect the Truths," and "In Renewal, Piecemeal Approach Can't Work").[33] These editorials emphasized the widespread blight in the area, and the consultants predicted a dramatic increase in the tax base of the project area within two years of acquisition.[34]

Citizens had one last moment to address their concerns at the city council meeting on June 27. Peters's group submitted a ten-and-a-half-page letter that described the plan as being "in reckless disregard of the human rights of your citizens affected" and one that would pose risks in the loss of "present substantial tax revenues." While his letter outlined additional critiques, including the fact that contracts had yet to be issued for the use of the land, his committee emphasized concerns with the "standards employed in the study of blight." He pressed the city council for another hearing "at which evidence would be given on the actual condition of buildings in the area." Yet when the city council voted unanimously to approve the project, it did so without holding additional public meetings or, as far as we can tell, ever providing the requested survey data to local citizens.[35] Despite Peters's continued efforts to block the project, negotiations with property owners commenced on September 1, with the Easton Redevelopment Authority obtaining the "right to

FIG. 7. *Lehigh-Washington Streets Demolition.* From the "Annual Report of the City of Easton, 1967–68," 69. Courtesy of the city of Easton PA.

possession" by December 9, 1963.[36] Demolition began the next year, and the area was cleared by the end of 1967.[37]

This project was controversial even after its completion. The ERA encountered "seemingly endless difficulties finding buyers" for the land, which remained empty for years. In the end, the city redeveloped most of the area as a series of public housing projects for the elderly, resulting in a decided loss of tax revenue (rather than the tenfold increase that had been promised).[38]

Competing Languages of Blight

The residents of Easton we met at Sami's bar were certainly correct in their belief that the city used the language of blight to describe the former Lebanese neighborhood and justify its demolition and that they were not alone. Easton was following a national trend. Since the first half of the twentieth century, Americans who were worried about a perceived rampant urban decline identified blight as the main enemy of the city.[39] By the 1930s local leaders concerned with the economic health of their city centers cited the "same litany of ills—declining population, dilapidated neighborhoods, declining property values and declining revenues from commercial and industrial sites, snarled traffic."[40] Across the country, urban planners, officials, and citizens determined that physical rejuvenation of the urban core would address these problems. Conflict emerged over how to proceed. Social workers and some urban leaders pushed for public housing, while real estate representatives promoted private enterprise. The federal government became a central actor in this process with the Housing Act of 1949, which historian Alexander von Hoffman has described as a failed compromise, the product of "seven years of bitter legislative stalemate and a shotgun wedding between enemy lobbying goals," or even as a victory for real estate company interests.[41] Title I of the act provided $1 billion in loans to eliminate slums through rebuilding. Localities received federal funds and the power of eminent domain to help them purchase and clear lands that would be earmarked for sale at a reduced cost to private developers who, it was hoped, would be enticed to rebuild.

In Easton city reports and in our discussions with former officials, concerns about the spread of "blight" were prominent. The Easton Redevelopment Authority's *Questions and Answers on Urban Renewal*, a Xeroxed pamphlet distributed through the Citizens Advisory Committee in 1963, referred to blight as a "sickness that plagues," a condition where "a single dilapidated building . . . spread[s] the infection to the surrounding area." Conveying the need to "beautify" and "revitalize" Easton, city reports and brochures attempted to show the tremendous possibilities of urban renewal programs. These publications communicated a great sense of optimism, replete with images of a new, airy, utopian version of downtown Easton with modern, high-rise buildings. Artists' renditions of the "renewed" Easton were contrasted with illustrations of "dilapidated dwellings," "junk and weed infested yards," "bleak depressing environments," and the "absence of adequate sanitation," conditions that all contributed to Easton's "blighted" state.[42]

This language was in some ways preordained by federal policy. Since a primary goal of Title I of the Housing Act of 1949 was to eliminate slums or blighted areas, localities could obtain the federal funds only after demonstrating the existence of "blight." However, the federal acts never clearly defined the terms "slum" and "blighted areas." Even an official charged with formulating housing standards and measures stated in the

Artist's concept of proposed development of S. Third Street, between Ferry and Washington Streets. Commercial complex proposed by Jack and George Chartier (Fairway Developers, Inc.), consists of motel, office building, department store, shopping mall, and theater.

FIG. 8. Radical changes proposed by developers. From "Artist's Concept of Proposed Development of South Third Street," 1970–1971 Annual Report, city of Easton PA, 20. Courtesy of the city of Easton PA.

1950s that blight "refers to not one characteristic or condition. . . . Instead, it covers a fairly wide range of conditions and characteristics." To qualify, a "blighted" area needed to have both building and environmental deficiencies: "At least 20 percent of the buildings in the area must contain one or more building deficiencies, and the area must contain at least two environmental deficiencies." The list of qualifying "environmental deficiencies" was especially vague and subjective, and it included such characteristics as overcrowding; improper location of structures; excessive dwelling unit density; conversions to incompatible types of uses, such as rooming houses among family dwellings; obsolete building types; detrimental land uses or conditions, such as incompatible uses, structures in mixed use, or adverse influences from noise, smoke, or fumes; and unsafe, congested, poorly designed, or otherwise deficient streets.[43]

As we have seen, most city residents who opposed the project underscored the neighborhood's *physical structures* and interpreted blight to be a measure of building quality. Easton's official reports, on the other hand, were highly variable. Private consulting firms invariably attempted to quantify the amounts of blight found across the city. The use of numbers and percentages and of phrases such as "intensity of blight" added an air of scientific rationality to the city's redevelopment programs. And yet these very measures were extremely inconsistent across the different reports produced for city government, in part because blight was defined in different ways. The City Planning Commission's 1956 "Revised Comprehensive General Plan" stated, "Blight in the City is not widespread. In most cases it is confined to pockets throughout the City, except in Wards 5 [the location of the Lehigh-Washington project], 11 and 12 where the intensity of blight is over 35%."[44]

When the ERA first narrowed its sights on the Lehigh-Washington Street section of Ward 5, it contracted Morris Knowles, Inc., an engineering consulting firm, to conduct a substandard dwelling survey in 1960. This survey revealed quite different figures. It recommended that only 16 percent of the 149 dwellings surveyed (or 24 buildings) be considered for "repair or demolition," not the "over 35%" found in the 1956 plan.[45] This hardly seemed to justify the wholesale demolition of the entire neighborhood, and it is perhaps no surprise that the redevelopment proponents could not locate this survey during the single public hearing on the proposal. It never resurfaced publicly despite the fact that Pastor Peters's working group in particular continued to question the grounds on which the "blight" label had been based, and we were surprised to find it in the city archives.

A mere two years later, neighborhood blight was apparently spreading. The 1962 *Annual Report* of the city of Easton noted that "110 of the 152 buildings" (72.4 percent) in the Lehigh-Washington Street area contained "one or more deficiencies" warranting clearance.[46] But that same year, consultants at Morris Knowles argued that blight in the area had reached a remarkable 99.9 percent. The firm's 1962 land use plan admits that such a dramatic shift in the degree of blight was partly due to changing categories in the census between 1950 and 1960. According to Morris Knowles, the 1950 census "did not list a category to show where 'deterioration' was taking place." "'Deterioration,'" the report noted, "is an impor-

Lehigh Street—Satisfactory

Jefferson Street—Unsatisfactory

FIG. 9. *Lehigh Street: Satisfactory*. From "A Report on the Comprehensive General Plan of the City of Easton, PA—1957," unpublished report by the City of Easton Planning Commission, 20. Courtesy of the city of Easton PA.

tant criterion under the new concepts of current Federal programs. As a result, only major areas of dilapidation could be pinpointed" in 1950.[47] The addition of the new category "deteriorating" or "housing in need of more repair than would be provided in the course of regular maintenance" to the already existing categories "sound" and "dilapidated" had the effect of increasing the quantity of blighted structures.[48] According to these new criteria, Ward 5 had 239 deteriorating and 305 dilapidated homes, or 544 (99.9 percent) of the 547 total units.[49] Looking more closely at the 1962 *Annual Report*, we find yet another explanation for the ever-shifting measurements. While 72.4 percent of the buildings had "one or more deficiencies," the report noted that "the entire area contains *environmental deficiencies*, such as improper conversions, to a degree and extent that almost total clearance is necessary."[50]

City reports offered different measures of blight and thus different rationales for demolition from one year to the next. At times, demolition was justified by a quantification of the degree of deterioration and dilapidation of the neighborhood's *structures*, while other reports argued that the *environmental* deficiencies were extensive enough to warrant complete clearance. Sometimes the same data could be spun in different directions according to official whims. An image of a portion of Lehigh Street appears in the Easton City Planning Commission's "A Report on the Comprehensive General Plan of the City of Easton PA—1957" as an example of "satisfactory" housing, in contrast with the "blighted" housing on Jefferson Street slated that year for demolition.[51] That same city block was deemed blighted a few years later and razed as part of the Lehigh-Washington Street project.

By the end of June 1963 city council members were unanimous in their condemnation of the neighborhood, and in the bill they signed, they cited deficiencies in "over 75 percent" of the structures, describing the neighborhood as a "blighted area . . . and a menace to the safety, health, and welfare" of both its inhabitants and the city as a whole, even though the building survey had recommended demolishing only a fraction of the structures.[52] The question remains: If the buildings were in fact in reasonable shape, what else about this section of the city drew the attention of city leaders?

Race, Ethnicity, and Other "Deficiencies"

RACHEL: I am curious as to why specific areas of the city were chosen and not others. . . .

FORMER MAYOR: They were slums! Abject slums!

RACHEL: What was wrong with them?

MAYOR: What do you mean, what was wrong with them? They had a lot of crime, a lot of fires, they had a lot of problems, a lot of delinquency . . . of all kinds.

RACHEL: Really. And the building structures were in bad physical condition as well?

MAYOR: Absolutely. In effect, what you're doing is condemning the property.[53]

Through our close reading of city reports and interviews with former residents, it became apparent that aspects of the neighborhood aside from its deteriorating physical structures likely drew the attention of city leaders. Its very foreignness, its unusual integration of different races, sometimes in the same building, the mixing of generations in the Lebanese homes, and perhaps the custom of creating separate apartments for extended family members or lodgers (the improper conversions cited above) all defied city norms. Some interviewees felt that city officials thought that it was the people themselves, not the properties, who were "blighted." As Ellen shouted at Sami's Place that night, "They made us out to be dirt, but we're not!" Although most Lebanese-origin interviewees did not remark on an anti-Lebanese prejudice, some black interviewees told us they felt that this sentiment had been fairly widespread among the city elite. Some Lebanese indicated a nativist flavor to local politics, however. An elderly man explained it this way:

> Urban renewal was a disaster, very much a disaster, and it devastated our people, tore us apart. We were forced to move out. . . . What they wanted was to get rid of us, to integrate us into American society, but we were Americans anyway. We went to school, you know, most of our people who graduated there became magistrates, lawyers, doctors. . . . All of a sudden you're supposed to lose your culture and your heritage because it's somebody's idea to knock this out?

Anthony, an eighty-five-year-old Lebanese man, met with us at his office in city hall. He had launched a valiant fight against the renewal projects some forty years before we met. When we asked if he thought any anti-Lebanese prejudice played a factor in the dismantling of the neighborhood, he responded:

> Very definitely! At that time, they're foreigners and didn't belong in this country. A lot of people looked down on them because they're foreigners . . . They had no regard . . . I'm not saying everybody, but the powers that be that were in power, they'd destroy any foreign neighborhood, they looked down on nationalities . . . Now, believe me, they know who you are, what nationality you are. Inside, a lot of them haven't gotten over that, you know what I'm talking about? They'll be nice to you and all that, but 'He's a *Syrian*,' and that happens to all nationalities.

Did Easton officials target the Lehigh-Washington Street area due to its *Lebanese* character? Despite the area's common designation as the "Lebanese" neighborhood, as Syrian Town, the documentary record is noticeably silent on this characteristic of this part of town. Newspaper articles and official city reports on the project invariably referred to the area by its official designation, the Lehigh-Washington Street project (even though whole files in city archives are labeled with the shorthand "Lebanese," and one African American woman in her seventies explained to us that "Lehigh-Washington" was merely a "code word" for Lebanese). City consultants, however, had scrutinized the town's social makeup closely. A 1964 report titled "Population Characteristics" advocated "[taking] physical, economic, social, and political aspects of society into consideration" when deciding to implement "community renewal objectives." This report was designed to determine the existence of undesirable social elements in the city of Easton. Encouraging the city to assess qualities of citizens in making urban renewal decisions, the report introduced a "Ward Rating System." This rating system ranked Easton's twelve wards using first through fourth quartiles on ten different population features, including income, family size, education, and employment. The report deemed populations of more affluent wards more desirable than those in low-income wards. Ward 5, the ward of the former Lebanese neighborhood, ranked in the bottom quartiles of all but one population feature.[54]

But nowhere were the ward's unique *cultural* features discussed. It sometimes appeared that report writers had actively silenced any discussion of ethnicity. For example, the "Minorities Group" report asserted that the city's only visible minority group was "nonwhite." The report acknowledged the city's large Italian-origin population but discounted it. "While the population is 11 percent Italian origin, they are largely 2nd and 3rd generation, dispersed in the city, with concentrations in Wards 6 and 8," the report noted, although no ward's population exceeded 25 percent Italian origin. Why, one wonders, was the city's high Lebanese component not also mentioned here? The report stated that because there were "no significant nationality groups in Easton for minority consideration," it would highlight the city's "Negro" population, the "only significant minority group."[55] And yet the city's "Housing Conditions" report, published that same year, noted a high concentration of *foreigners* in Ward 5. This emerged only indirectly in an explanation of the ward's unusual age composition, with a quarter of the population under age twelve and people over age forty-five comprising approximately 40 percent of the total. This unusual composition, the report stated, likely stemmed from the fact that "part of the population [could] be categorized as new arrivals. Families thus tend[ed] to be large and include both young children and grandparents."[56] These "new arrivals" were clearly recent immigrants from Lebanon and relatives of existing ward residents. According to our research and that of others, the extended family household composition was typical in the homes of neighborhood Lebanese residents.[57] Thus, the Lebanese character of Ward 5 only appears in official reports in this masked fashion.

The neighborhood's racial characteristics are another story altogether. Ample studies have shown that federal renewal programs and policies were not race neutral; the very development of Easton's suburbs was facilitated by policies and practices of the Federal Housing Administration (FHA), which encouraged the Home Owners' Loan Corporation's (HOLC) notorious neighborhood rating system to determine the creditworthiness of its housing. This rating system was overtly racist, and it fostered white flight, disinvestment in urban centers, and residential segregation. FHA guidelines even instructed realtors and land developers that "if a neighborhood is to retain stability it is necessary that properties shall continue to be occupied by the same social and racial classes."[58]

The new Housing Acts of 1949 and 1954 only exacerbated existing housing discrimination nationally, as several studies have documented.[59] Slum clearance became known as "Negro clearance," for people of color were disproportionately displaced by highway and renewal projects. Overall, two-thirds of the people uprooted by such projects were nonwhites.[60] Urban renewal has been described as presenting a "triple threat" to people of color: it displaced them from desirable neighborhoods, reduced the supply of housing open to them, and forced the breakup of integrated neighborhoods.[61] Already by 1959 the Commission on Civil Rights reported that urban renewal was "accentuating patterns of clearcut racial separation."[62]

Was the Lehigh-Washington Street area targeted for its *racial* composition? We have noted that the neighborhood's racial integration was a feature that stands out quite positively in popular accounts today. What public statements on the Lehigh-Washington Street project never mention, and what internal city reports note often, is the fact that the neighborhood had the city's highest concentration of people of color. The 1960 census showed an overall decline in the city's population by roughly 10 percent, from 35,632 to 31,955, and this decline was greatest in the central city wards. But consultants' reports also indicated that the city's population of "Negroes" was increasing, from 1.5 percent in 1950 to 4.0 percent in 1960.[63] These same reports also demonstrated that this was higher than the percentage of nonwhites in the nearby cities of Allentown and Bethlehem, which were .77 and 1.7 percent "Negro" in 1960. This was a very white area of the country: it should also be pointed out that the numbers of "nonwhites" in Easton were far greater than in adjacent suburban towns such as Forks, Nazareth, and Palmer, which had grand totals of one, one, and zero nonwhite individuals in 1960, respectively.[64] What is more, the city's "Negro" population was not evenly distributed; rather, it was concentrated on the Lehigh River's south side and in a few downtown wards, notably Ward 1, with 10.4 percent; Ward 6, with 4.0 percent; and Ward 5, the locus of the Lehigh-Washington Street project, with 27.1 percent of the residents.[65] Was this entirely coincidental?

Easton's branch of the NAACP did not think so, and it protested the project on these grounds. These protests were part of a much wider effort the organization mounted to oppose housing discrimination in the city. The NAACP also targeted the membership of the Easton Redevelopment Authority. In early 1963, for instance, the NAACP opposed the ERA's appointment of Hugh Moore, Jr.[66] Moore was the founder and former chairman of the board of the Dixie Cup company, one of the area's most successful businesses. He was also an architect and local philanthropist who, on the day of his appointment to the ERA, had presented his final gift to the city of Easton in the form of land to create a recreational area along the Lehigh River (now known as Hugh Moore Park).[67] Perhaps not unrelated is the fact that Moore was also the designer of the award-winning Union Streets project, one highly lauded in city reports and one that NAACP president Thomas Bright later blamed for the eviction of a large number of black families.[68] The NAACP argued that it was time to have an African American on the authority board, and it raised the issue of the repeated relocations of the city's black population:

All over the Nation, and here in Easton, Negro families have been pushed and shoved about to make room for redevelopment projects.

We are not opposed to progress, but such progress too often has come about at very high cost and with great suffering to Negro families. . . . There is no reason why a Negro should not have been appointed to this board. Negro citizens have a greater stake in redevelopment plans than any other group in Easton, and they deserve an adequate voice in the decisions which are made.[69]

Moore made public his response to the NAACP challenge. He noted that the Citizen Advisory Committee had been expanded to twenty members, including Bright. He added that "too often these advisory committees are 'paper committees' created to fulfill requirements of laws related to urban renewal. So long as I am on the authority, this will not be the case."[70] It is unclear what power members of that committee held, if any.

Further concerns about the impact of the Lehigh-Washington renewal plan on the local black community were raised at an NAACP meeting the following month. An *Easton Express* editorial laid bare some of these concerns. In the renewal area, it reported, "80 white and 32 Negro families will have to be resettled." With the community redevelopment program moving into "high gear," the editorial continued, and with its "chief emphasis on supplanting 'blight' with income-generating and tax-producing land uses, the housing squeeze on the bottom-income groups . . . is bound to increase." The editorial noted that the city's black resident, "in displacement from private housing by renewal programs, does not have the freedom of movement available to dispossessed whites. He carries the burden of racial prejudice as well as the economic disadvantage."[71]

Thomas Bright continued to press city officials. He invited Joseph C. Dowell, executive director of the ERA, to an NAACP branch meeting to answer questions about the proposed project. Many African Americans, he pointed out, "give up homes under the authority redevelopment program and are unable to obtain homes in the better areas of Easton." In response to a suggestion that "in many cases Negroes are unable to buy homes in the better sections because they often work at low paying jobs, and can't obtain bank loans as a result," Bright stated, "We are going to stop sugar-coating these issues and start presenting [them] as they actually are."[72]

The NAACP organized several rallies over the course of the summer to protest "poor housing opportunities" and alleged job discrimination in private business and city and county government.[73] It held several rallies and picketed city hall. One of the signs displayed at the city hall rally stated, "Why Can't I Live on College Hill?," citing the elite all-white neighborhood overlooking downtown.[74] Housing too was on the minds of local participants in the August 1963 march on Washington, DC. The *Easton Express* quoted Bright as saying, "Easton needs to wake up. Jobs and housing for our Negroes are bad problems." Another participant in the march, Mrs. Robert Miller, a registered nurse, stated, "Does Easton have discrimination? Oh yes, right where it hurts the most—in housing, particularly."[75]

We have no clear evidence that the Easton Redevelopment Authority targeted the Lehigh-Washington Street area intentionally to reduce the number of nonwhites living in the downtown business district. Nevertheless, this was the ultimate result. By 1965, in the midst of the Lehigh-Washington Street removals, that project and the preceding projects for Union and Jefferson Streets had "accelerated the movement of the Negro to the South Side" (i.e., to the other side of the Lehigh River; see map 1). Another study found that due to the removals of populations induced by demolitions associated with the previous three redevelopment projects (Canal Street, Union Street, and Jefferson Street), "over half of the Negro population of Easton is now in the 4 wards south of the Lehigh River." Yet it is unclear from this report if this was viewed as a success or a failure, for report language indicates that its authors found the presence of minority residents to be a detriment to an area, finding that by 1965, the only areas of "severe concentration" of African Americans were in Ward 11.[76]

City leaders rarely discussed in public the ethnic and racial composition of the neighborhood they planned to obliterate. However, they often described the area as a "slum," as we see in the interview with a former city mayor quoted above. Even the *Easton Express*, which consistently held pro-redevelopment positions, at one point noted that "blight" is just another euphemism for "slum" and a way to index the "Negro" parts of town.[77] Such a position seems to be confirmed by a statement a former redevelopment-era mayor made to us about the project. "The Lehigh-

Washington Street project," he explained, "was quite controversial because that happened to be the area where most of the Lebanese immigrants lived. And many of them were well-to-do, and they did not have to live in the . . . you know, an area like that."[78] We imagined that the word he was searching for was "ghetto" or "slum." What he seemed to be trying to tell us is that the Lebanese should not have stayed on living with blacks in the city center. Was it the neighborhood's black population or the *mixture* of people that city officials disliked? We may never know. In a letter to the paper following the three-hour-long public hearing on the project at the end of May 1963, though, Hugh Moore, Jr., the member of the Easton Redevelopment Authority who had been condemned by the president of the NAACP, raised questions about the neighborhood's integrated nature. He referred to the people to be displaced as "national, religious, racial or culturally motivated groups." He continued, "Although I feel that diversity of national origins, beliefs and cultures is an enrichment of American life, it hardly seems a healthy influence as it exists in the Lehigh-Washington Street section." He added that he wanted to achieve "an *attractive* urban environment."[79]

Conclusion

In 1960s Easton, "blight" was a multivocal label that held different meanings to parties debating the Lehigh-Washington Street renewal project. In the popular understanding, "blight" indicated the physical decay of neighborhood structures. Neighborhood residents consistently challenged the project on the grounds that the buildings were solid and well maintained. This meaning was sometimes the intent in official usage as well, although reports using this more mainstream definition still found highly variable measurements of "blight" from one year to the next. Ultimately, however, city officials defended the demolition of the neighborhood on wholly different grounds: the existence of "environmental deficiencies," such as "improper conversions" and "crowded conditions," features that allowed them to claim that the targeted area was entirely "blighted." This concern, perhaps with the burgeoning multigenerational households that typified some of the residences, was a common one for bourgeois reformers who linked progress to a "single concept of family housing" rooted in an "autonomous nuclear family."[80] But even this usage masked another key concern, namely, the neighborhood's social characteristics and, in particular, its ethnic and racial composition. Close scrutiny of city documents reveals that officials had tremendous interest in the racial composition of the neighborhood. This open secret emerges in plain detail in internal reports, but it is never associated with the Lehigh-Washington Street project in forums or literature meant for the wider public.

It is ultimately in this gap between different languages of blight that real miscommunication occurred, creating the sense of betrayal that many of the town's citizens still feel today. The fact that the city leaders never made public their 1960 building survey and did not hold additional public hearings suggests that officials had something to hide. They certainly could have clarified the grounds on which the neighborhood "blight" label was based or educated the public as to which environmental deficiencies were so alarming.

Easton officials were certainly not alone in their quest to search out and destroy "blight." To obtain federal funds under Title I of the Housing Act of 1949, Local Housing Authorities (LHAS) in towns of all sizes had to locate and demonstrate the presence of "blight." As subsequent housing acts increased the proportion of costs borne by the federal government, these programs became very attractive to officials in smaller cities such as Easton. As *The Citizen's Guide to Urban Renewal* reports, the Housing Act of 1961's reduction of the local financial burden to just 25 percent of costs "made the program almost irresistible for any city that wishe[d] to face up to the problems of blight."[81]

Yet this "blight" was not the easily measured and quantifiable physical attribute that city reports suggest. Localities hired teams of engineers, social scientists, and other "experts" to help them identify how to best garner federal funds. But federal guidelines were so vague that the conclusions of ostensibly scientific studies—even those prepared in the same year—varied widely. As historian Mark Gelfand writes, "Severe distortions were created in the slum clearance process. . . . Areas that could not objectively be called blighted were nonetheless demolished because their desirable locations made them ripe for 'higher uses' such as office buildings and civic centers."[82] This was the case in Easton, as well as in Boston's West and South Ends and San Francisco's Western Addition, where city planners justified renewal by painting pictures of social decay. In doing so, they attacked well-working communities, much like the neighborhoods Herbert Gans and John Mollenkopf describe as "urban villages" that were characterized by "intense ethnic community life" centered around churches, shops, and taverns.[83]

It is no wonder that the former residents we interviewed were confused and continue to defend the quality of their neighborhood's housing stock with passion forty years after the fact. Whether or not this was a physically inferior, so-called blighted neighborhood was a pivotal and loaded question of vital import when the project was under consideration, and it remains one to many people today. This case reminds us that "production of space" is always intertwined with the workings of power; often, the struggle over different lifestyles, behaviors, and practices is manifested by struggles over space.[84] We could see the removal of a part of town in which inhabitants had been engaged in "place-making practices" for decades as an extreme example of such a struggle, and we could perceive the outright removal of places as an effort to eradicate whole ways of life. For among the lasting legacies of urban renewal projects are their social consequences, seen here in terms of our interviewees' frustration, disillusionment with city government, and sense of being completely bypassed by the political process.

As former residents lament the process that took their homes from them, what they seem to miss the most about their neighborhood are the dense interpersonal ties they had there. They miss their ability to interact on a daily basis with people from a variety of ethnic and racial backgrounds, something lacking in their lives in the contemporary era, as we elaborate in the following chapters. In dismantling Syrian Town, Easton's powerful political leaders, not unlike the progressive, future-minded "radicals" who dismantled Eastwick outside of Philadelphia, attacked an integrated community and accelerated processes of segregation.[85] It is to this quality of the neighborhood—its racial and ethnic diversity—and the ways speakers relate to it in their stories that we now turn.

3. Narrating Diversity

In those days, the Lebanese, the Jews, the Italians, the Afro-Americans . . . all lived mixed, one right after the other.

AGATHA, a Lebanese woman

I had a lot of Lebanese friends, Lebanese, Syrian, blacks, everything.

JERRY, a black man

And you might be sitting there at the table eating tomato sandwiches, and you got a black friend there, a Lebanese friend, Italian friend, a . . . you know. . . . Who knows, that was all one big happy family.

LARRY, an Italian man

When people described their neighborhood to us at bars and during reunions and interviews, they emphasized its unity, describing it as close-knit, a "happy family," narrating it through a litany of ethnic labels ("Lebanese," "Syrian," "Italian"), as the passages above illustrate. When we heard these statements, we were struck by what seemed to us an intriguing tension in our speakers' stories: on the one hand, they emphasized the harmonious "mixed" nature of neighborhood sociality; on the other hand, they did so in narratives so ethnically marked that they sometimes felt jarring to us. This chapter explores the semiotics of ethnic labeling in these narratives. We consider what kind of social world they relate; what speakers are telling us about salient racial, ethnic, class, and other distinctions in 1940s–1960s Easton; and how their narratives reflect the contrasting contemporary social divisions in which they are embedded today. We will argue that along with denoting ethnic diversity, the labels are significant in that they index a certain kind of *place*, indirectly signaling a class divide characterizing the wider cityscape.

A Multiethnic Family

Over and over we heard people discuss their neighbors as members of a single community and their bygone neighborhood as a place where people looked after each other. When we interviewed Agatha, an eighty-nine-year-old Lebanese woman, she was living in a tiny apartment for seniors overlooking a vast parking lot. Her ground-floor living room was chock-full: there was a small Jesus figurine in the corner, and lace doilies on every surface were covered with framed photos of relatives. She picked up the photo of her mother every time she mentioned her. She had been a sharp dresser and was proud of it. While talking about her favorite dress shop, owned by a local family, she interrupted her own story to add the following:

> They were one of the best, they were a wonderful family. See, I'm Lebanese, they were Jewish. In those days, the Lebanese, the Jews, the Italians, the Afro-Americans . . . all lived mixed, one right after the other. Now, we went to each other's funerals, we went to each other's weddings, we were there for each other . . . and that is something that I will never forget. As I grew up, the world changed, you know, everything changed.

During a reunion we taped a group of women as they met and talked about past times. Carol, in her late fifties, brought her eighty-two-year-old mother, Pam, of Sicilian descent. Also in the group were Linda, seventy-five years old and of Irish and Welsh descent, and Vera, an octogenarian of Albanian ancestry. At one point, Carol prompted a new line of discussion:

> CAROL: You told me stories where everybody looked out for each other.
> PAM: Yeah, they did.
> LINDA: Oh yeah, all the time. Everybody watched each other.
> CAROL: It didn't matter if you were a child of the Italians, Lebanese, black, whatever.

PAM: No, it made no difference in those days.

LINDA: *No.*

PAM: Not like today.

VERA: As long as you treated us fine, then you were fine. And everybody got along. I always hated it when they got rid of the Lebanese.

We could assume that these portrayals of harmonious relations between the neighborhood's subgroups were mainly shaped by the speakers' overwhelming nostalgia for their lost neighborhood or that the elderly speakers were emphasizing what they thought we wanted to hear. However, not all stories we heard were positive. Many people reported microlevel residential segregation, for instance. Although he described his elementary school as "a melting pot," eighty-four-year-old Jerry was also quick to point out the segregated nature of the city as a whole in the past: "Being black, we weren't allowed in many places." In another interview, he delineated the blocks that were open to blacks and the blocks they couldn't live on. We began asking people of other backgrounds about this, and they concurred. Gloria, the octogenarian of English and German descent who married a Sicilian man, responded as follows:

ALS: So there were little subneighborhoods within the neighborhood?

GLORIA: Yeah. Was [an] Italian section, Lebanese section. And I . . . I don't know about . . . there was black people over I think, maybe there were on Canal Street, I'm not really sure. But they all blended in with us. You see how Mark is? That's the way everybody was, so friendly and so nice.

Pam also noted microsegregation, particularly between Italians and Lebanese:

And on our street, in Washington Street, the whole one side, the Lehigh Street, down lower, that was all Lebanese. Nothing but Lebanese lived there. They owned that section. So the Lebanese came out to the front of Washington Street. That's as far as they got, because the Italians had the right side. And then . . . all the way down 5th Street was Italian, big 5th Street hill, they were Italian, then they were Italian on 4th Street, and a few Lebanese had got in there.

Despite concentrations of people of similar backgrounds on certain blocks, on another level the neighborhood as a whole was conceived of as one community. While Jerry was the most forthright about antiblack discrimination in the past, perhaps reflecting his long-standing involvement in the local chapter of the NAACP, he also claimed that there was tremendous integration:

AE: But you all went to school together.
JERRY: Yeah, that was a melting pot. Everything, *all* nationalities went to Taylor School.
AE: Yeah.
JERRY: Taylor School was the first integrated school, I think, in the United States, because everybody went there [*chuckling*].
AE: Did you all get along?
JERRY: Oh yeah, we all got along. I mean, we, you know, like kids, you fist-fought, you know, but nobody was for, no group was for any special group. You had just as many people rooting for you to win as for your opponents to beat you up, you know?

On another occasion, Jerry told us: "Italian and black, we all lived together. I picked up a little Italian, we all lived together." Pam, too, told us: "We didn't care where we lived, we were all friendly, we were all friendly, and we all loved each other." Mark concurred. He was one of the most active of the reunion organizers, and he regularly sent us names of additional people to invite. On one occasion, in response to his depiction of the neighborhood as "a clustered community living close together," we responded that it sounded like a real community. His reply was swift: "Oh *yeah*, like I *said*, we all played together. Eddie Berkat [Lebanese coorganizer of the reunion], that guy who was there, there were no prejudices, we all got along *too* well."

Larry, of Italian descent, was interviewed in his home by a college student who was of Italian ancestry herself. After she commenced the ninety-minute interview with a quick neutral question, he launched into a long monologue:

> STUDENT: So, can you describe your experience growing up or living in Easton?
>
> LARRY: I grew up right on South 5th Street [part of the renewal area]. That area was a large Italian community. Between 3rd Street and 6th Street and the Lehigh River and Northampton Street there was an Italian community, a Lebanese community, and a Lebanese community [sic]. And we all grew up together. There was no discrimination, nobody, no color or religion or anything. Everybody grew up together in that area.

Later on in the interview, the student asked specifically about the neighborhood's diversity:

> STUDENT: Um, I know you kind of touched on this before a little bit, about sort of the diversity in the neighborhood. Could you talk about that some more? Especially particularly like the Italian community's place within this larger ethnic community.
>
> LARRY: We, like I said, it was one happy family, we didn't . . . we didn't have color. There was, there was a lot of Jewish people, there was a lot of oh uh Lebanese people. Matter of fact, I just got off the phone with one of, uh, a Lebanese fellow that I know, he's also an attorney. Still, that area down there, when they tore that area down they ripped out the Lebanese community, the Italian community, the black community, and they scattered them all over. [We omit a long passage in which he discusses how everybody now lives in the suburbs.] But we, we used to, you know, everybody got fed. You didn't have much, but you shared it. And you might be sitting there at the table eating tomato sandwiches, and you got a black friend there, a Lebanese friend, Italian friend, a—you know—who knows, that was all one big happy family.

We can see several common themes from these passages. People talk of the neighborhood as a "melting pot" composed of "all nationalities." They portray interethnic intimacy, as in Larry's depiction of friends of different backgrounds eating lunch together and when he said, "Everybody grew up together in that area." It was a "big happy family." What was significant to Agatha was how everybody attended "each other's funerals."

We also can observe a pervasive use of ethnonyms. Not only is everyone associated with an ethnonym, but these labels are employed so liberally that they were almost more important than or certainly as important as people's names. At meetings, people often interrupted their stories to identify the ethnicities of the people involved. We can see this in Agatha's quick shift from discussing her favorite dress shop to outlining in detail the dress shop owner's ancestry and the neighborhood's diverse composition. We did not ask for this information at the start of the interviews. The attorney Larry references is described first as Lebanese and then as an attorney. In our taped interview, Agatha regularly interrupted herself to include her characters' ethnic affiliation: "The Walkers! The Walkers was Afro-American, and they had a home which was gorgeous." In a similar interruption, another man told us, "John, the pharmacist at Ball's Apothecary—he's Lebanese—his cousin used to be a doctor."

Along with sections of city blocks and individuals, even shops and churches had ethnic affiliations, and people talked about "their" bakery and "their" church in such a way that ethnic affiliation was implied. The Catholic Church community was ethnically segregated, as Larry explained:

> When I was younger, St. Anthony's was the Italian church, St. Bernard's was the Irish church, St. Joseph's was the German church, St. Michael's was the Lithuanian church, Holy Name was the Ukrainian church, Our Lady of Lebanon was the Lebanese church—they're all Catholic churches, but they all had their own specific thing and a lot of times if you went to church, say you went to St. Bernard's church, you were frowned upon: if you were Italian, you should go to St. Anthony's.

The need to attach an ethnic label to individuals was so great that the absence of a label could completely derail a conversation. The conversation with Carol, Pam, and Vera became almost comedic when Linda kept interrupting Vera's story, shouting, "Was she Greek?!" "What, yes, she lived on . . ." "No . . . she was Greek?" "What?" "What was her *nationality*, was she *Greek*?"

What does it mean to identify everyone first and foremost by ethnicity? How can a community be both united and divided at the same time? Might the ethnic labels serve to index some other salient social distinction, such as race? A close look at ethnonyms reveals a great deal about social distinctions relevant in 1940s–1960s neighborhood life and their meanings today.

Local Ethnonymic Usage

Anthropologists often commence their studies of culturally complex communities with explorations of the semiotics of labels associated with the classification of populations.[1] Even single ethnonyms merit close analysis, with key terms taking on different meanings depending on conversational context.[2] As Frank Proschan writes, "Through closely focused attention to the detailed operations of ethnonymic systems in social and conversational contexts, we may begin to discern how these models are conceived and instantiated in given settings."[3] In their discussion of whiteness, Sara Trechter and Mary Bucholtz defend works that take seriously such folk labels: "To invoke an identity category is not necessarily to fall into the trap of essentialism or reification. It may simply be sound anthropology. . . . If we are to do ethnographic justice to the people we study, we must use the categories that are meaningful to them."[4] In this study, doing so took some work, particularly since at first glance these were all familiar terms. Through further analysis, we found that the local idioms we encountered challenge scholarly categories and reveal the "gap" between the "certainty encompassed by experts' designations of 'racial' and the uncertainty or instability of deployments of the term by 'natives.'"[5]

According to our informants, people could be categorized by approximately a dozen ethnonyms. Interestingly, within this array of labels are some that in academic parlance would be considered "racial" labels ("black," "colored," "African American," "white"), while others were "ethnic" categories ("Lebanese," "Italian," "German," "Irish," "Lithuanian") that could also designate citizenship status ("American," "Italian," etc.), and still another was "religious" in basis ("Jewish"). These labels are clues to local understandings of the social world. Moreover, although they are rooted in overlapping criteria, it is important to note that they were employed by our interviewees in an unproblematic, either/or, what Thomas Eriksen describes as a "digital" fashion.[6] There did not seem to be any question in people's minds about this method of sorting people or their treatment of the categories as mutually exclusive.

We find it significant that we rarely encountered compound nationality-based terms, such as "Lebanese American," even though the people we met and most of the people they were discussing were American citizens. Our speakers were never concerned at all that the people they were describing as "Lebanese," "German," "Irish," or "Italian" were in fact Lebanese Americans, German Americans, and so forth. We rarely heard the word "American" throughout any of our interviews except in the compound label "African Americans." The label "white" was also exceedingly rare, as we develop further.

Some populations were designated by more than one ethnonym. It is common in multiethnic settings for people to employ different terms for self and for other; exonyms and autonyms do not always correspond, with outsiders' names for self often reproducing implicit or even quite explicit derogatory speech.[7] We found a variation on this pattern: speakers were most systematic in labeling their own group and used autonyms consistently. It was the exonyms that allowed for more variability, particularly regarding the two social groups that have experienced the most dramatic shifts in labeling, the Lebanese Americans and the African Americans. Because the neighborhood itself was labeled locally as Syrian Town, it is worth starting with the "Syrian" ethnonym.

Legal nomenclature for migrants from the Ottoman Empire varied widely in the United States until 1899, when immigration officials began employing the label "Syrian."[8] The vast majority of these migrants were Christian, and, consonant with Ottoman practice, residents of this multiethnic empire had self-identified according to religious affiliation.[9] "Syrian" became a preferred autonym for immigrants in the United States who used it to designate a "speaker of Arabic who was not a Muslim but a follower of one of the ancient Syrian Christian churches that still existed in the Near East."[10] "Syrians" became "Lebanese" sometime after Lebanon's independence (1946), when most of our speakers were teens or young adults. Lebanese interlocutors often pointed this out to us. One man explained, "They called us 'Syrians,' but that was inaccurate." Others told us, "They didn't call us 'Lebanese,' they called us 'Syrian.' They used to say this was a 'Syrian Town.' 'Goin' on down to the Syrian Town,' but we weren't Syrians." "Yeah, they used to call us Syrian Town. We're not Syrians." "Everybody said that's where the Syrians lived. That's how we knew it as. Never said 'Lebanese,' it was always 'Syrians.'"

Labels used to denote the black population followed a similar patterning. The changing labels for African Americans over the past several centuries (from "African" and "free" vs. "slave" to "colored," "Negro," "black," and "African American") is a topic of considerable scholarship, and the political dimensions of ethnonym choice, the coexistence of competing terms, and the changing patterns in in-group and out-group usage are the focus of active research.[11] As labels came to index negative stereotypes, new labels were promoted by the black elite, as in 1988, when Reverend Jesse Jackson publicly fostered the term "African American."[12] The arrival of new ethnonyms does not always mean the systematic extinction of old terms, however. One of John Baugh's informants reported to him that blacks are clear about which terms they believe are negative; positive terms are more dynamic and take time to enter the vernacular.[13] While our black interlocutors consistently employed "black," we heard a series of terms from the nonblack narrators, including "colored," "Afro-American," "African American," and "black." Yet our black interviewees were clear about which labels were appropriate for which era: when discussing a student-prepared volume of memories, a black woman explained that for a heading about a 1950s cheerleader, the correct label was "colored."

Inversely, non-Lebanese interviewees sometimes seemed confused when selecting a label for the Lebanese. Rosie, a black woman in her seventies, switched back and forth between the Lebanese and Syrian titles, perhaps as a strategy of inclusion, and in our experience, her fluency only faltered at these moments: "They demolished that . . . that . . . that Lebanese neighborhood, that one Syrian Lebanese neighborhood where their church was and everybody there." On another occasion, she reported, "He used to make up special orders of medicines for us black people and for Syrians and for Lebanese." Jerry was more aware of the distinction between autonym and exonym: "When I was a kid they used to call this Syrian Town, but there were no Syrians around here. They were Lebanese. Now why it got called Syrian Town I don't know."

We rarely heard "white" used as exonym or autonym. No people claimed this identity for themselves, and we only heard the term three times after dozens of hours of taped and casual interviews, and each time by black speakers. A black woman used it when asking us if we had encountered one of her classmates from elementary school: "My little white friend, Freddy, I'm still trying to find him." Jerry used it when discussing a beach that was later segregated: "There was a beach there that was where all black people went and there was white people went with us." The only other usage of "white" occurred in reference to a certain prostitution ring in the city, identified as "white slavery."

Finally, only a few individuals were not attached to an overt ethnic label. All of these individuals, in our view, appeared to be white and would probably be classified as members of an unmarked "American" group. We will return to this example when we discuss a normative notion of whiteness that the labels also index.

The Meaning of Ethnic Mentions

Ethnonymic usage presupposed a social world in which people could be sorted unproblematically into discrete "types." We would now like to consider what other social information is communicated by this usage. We might assume that presenting peoples as members of clear-cut, inherited categories is racializing, especially since one of the "types" is black. Moreover, this pattern follows two of the four projects of white racist culture that Jane Hill identifies for the twenty-first-century United States: the creation of a taxonomy of human types and the assignment of individuals and groups to these types.[14]

Covert racializing discourses, "which racialize without being denotationally explicit about race," are often found to be involved in the continued maintenance of racial distinctions and their material consequences.[15] The concept of indexicality is often a productive one in explicating how this works.[16] In her publications on language socialization, Elinor Ochs distinguishes direct from indirect indexicality.[17] In direct indexicality, there is an unmediated relation between "one or more linguistic forms and some contextual dimension." In indirect indexicality, "a feature of the communicated event is evoked indirectly through the indexing of some *other* feature of the communicative event. In these cases, the feature of the communicative event directly indexed is conventionally linked to and helps to constitute some second feature of the communicative context, such that the indexing of one evokes or indexes the other."[18] An illustration of these processes can be found in Jane Hill's work on Mock Spanish. In her view, when adopted by white native English speakers, Mock Spanish directly indexes a "positive colloquial persona" while indirectly presupposing a "deep background involving the reproduction and production of racist negative stereotypes of Spanish speakers."[19] Could the ethnic labels we heard be involved in indexing race?

We never heard individuals rank or organize these categories into a hierarchy, a third element of Hill's model and an important component of most definitions of race. As Hilary Parsons Dick and Kristina Wirtz assert, race marks some people as fundamentally and irredeemably dangerous and Other.[20] The lack of a hierarchizing tendency and the fact that speakers stressed a sense of community among neighborhood residents suggest that we will want to avoid imposing the scholarly category of "race" onto this nomenclature.

In addition, speakers did not seem to be commenting on the qualities of the people marked in this way, unlike the "evaluative narratives" documented by Anna De Fina.[21] These were not stories about the putative qualities of "Lebaneseness," for instance. But certainly these terms were not meaningless. We can safely say that this ethnonymic usage indicates a "continuous dichotomization," the persistence of boundaries between the social groups so identified.[22] In a Barthian approach to ethnicity, it is the existence of the labels themselves rather than differences in the behaviors of the people so defined that demonstrates the presence of ethnic groups.[23]

Because ethnicities exist in systems and salient identities may range in any one setting beyond what in the literature is termed "ethnic" to include or blur into distinctions and social institutions such as "kinship, clanship, and perhaps even nationality," analysis must start with local usage, "grounded in indigenously meaningful categories of social classification."[24] While we rarely heard the term "ethnicity," our interviewees sometimes used the term "ethnic," especially as a label for the neighborhood as a whole, as above when Gloria was talking about it in contrast to other parts of town.[25] But it was the term "nationality" that was used the most often in connection to the neighborhood's different types. These "ethnic" peoples had a "nationality," and our speakers employed this term in a fashion that was quite similar to contemporary scholarly usage of "ethnicity," to designate ethnic background or descent. For instance, at the climax of the chaotic Greek discussion, one of the women had shouted, "What was her *nationality*, was she *Greek*?" On another occasion, Jerry stated, "That was a melting pot. Everything, everybody, all *nationalities* went to Taylor School." Another speaker discussed the "mix of personalities, *nationalities* at Taylor School." While on a few occasions people used "nationality" to denote people of foreign national origins, this was rare.

Interestingly, the terms used to divide the neighborhood into subgroups, "Lebanese," "German," "Italian," and so forth, are also decidedly ambiguous. In using "Lebanese" rather than "Lebanese American," speakers employ a usage that is simultaneously divisive and unifying. While it distinguishes "nationalities" from each other, it does not distinguish American citizens from non-Americans or second- from first-generation immigrants. Boundaries between these groups are blurred, with parents and children, grandparents and recent arrivals united under a single term. This blurring could be viewed as purposefully inclusive: "Yes, some of us are citizens and some are not, but we are all one," it suggests. A similar point could be made regarding the local use of the term "nationality." By employing a fuzzy category, expanded so that it does not refer exclusively to the referent's legal or citizenship status and that does not clearly identify the grounds on which distinctions are being made, newer arrivals and the earlier immigrants are lumped together with the same ethnonym and are viewed as equivalent to other *kinds* of groups (religious, as in "Jews," and racial groups, as in "whites" and "blacks"). Syrian Town, then, comprised a distinct "community"; this was where the "ethnics" lived, the Lebanese, blacks, Jews, Italians, Greeks, Germans, and Irish. In this integrated, mixed community, everyone had a "nationality." Knowing who was which nationality was essential for locating individuals back in time, back into the prior social space, and thus in re-creating the neighborhood in people's minds.[26]

Looking Down on Syrian Town

In their discussion of semiotic processes of identification, Mary Bucholtz and Kira Hall write that "just as important as understanding *how* identities are formed is understanding *why* they are formed, the purpose for which particular semiotic processes are put to use."[27] We now turn from labels' referential meanings to their indexical significance. In her study of the use of "ethnic mentions" in Mexican immigrants' narratives, De Fina identifies a corpus of such stories that make evaluative statements about different ethnoracial populations. In these "argumentative stories," speakers are making a persuasive point orienting the hearer to certain conclusions about different types of people.[28] In addition to argumentative stories, De Fina notes instances where a speaker's use of ethnic labels is relevant in light of the story world, "conveying implicit assumptions about the way ethnicity determines relationships between social agents in the real world" without being the main point of the narrative.[29] The relevance, she says, depends on the speaker's relationship to the interactional world and/or the story world.

Narratives involving "ethnic mentions" are not necessarily making wider statements about the types of people mentioned in the stories, however, nor do they necessarily engage in processes of racialization. While we feel that the narratives we analyze are "argumentative," the persuasive points being made do not concern the specific types of people referenced but instead the qualities of the *neighborhood* under discussion. Our speakers reference ethnicity to make an argumentative point not about a specific ethnic group but about the *story world*, that is to say, Syrian Town in past times. Moreover, our work finds that through indexical associations, these ethnonyms are implicated in processes of "class-ification": by telling narratives rich in ethnonyms, our speakers directly index their former membership in an ethnically rich community and indirectly claim a particular class status. In order to understand our speakers' use of ethnic labels, then, we must explore both the story world in which they engaged (reminiscences about Syrian Town) and the interactional context during which they described the story world.

The interactional world relevance of our data was both to speak to us, the researchers of the old neighborhood (white women from College Hill), and to one another, neighbors reunited, returning to the story world: the Syrian Town of the past. In this context, the functioning of ethnicity *was* the argumentative point, made both directly and indirectly by our interviewees. Directly, they described the integrated nature of the place at that time. Indirectly, as seen in the vignettes above, they expressed the story world's integration, affectively, seamlessly reaching across ethnic "boundaries" in their behavior toward one another and using ethnic labels naturally as they described life in the past. The neighborhood as described by our speakers was populated by diverse "ethnic peoples," a diversity indexically presupposed by the labels themselves. Thus, in our example, ethnic labels model a certain kind of place, a specific neighborhood understood to be both diverse and integrated.

This place was also understood to be composed of hard-working families of modest means. When an elderly Lebanese woman, Dorothy, explained, "There weren't too many professionals, no, not there," Andrea asked if she'd describe the area as "working class." Her reply was immediate: "A lot of working-class people. Some of my best friends, they went to work in the factories when they were like thirteen and fourteen years old." The question of Syrian Town's economic standing in relation to other neighborhoods was sometimes discussed in a cryptic fashion, perhaps a legacy of the renewal era. For instance, one man stated, "Those homes on that side were a little older, but it wasn't that they were slum areas, they were just—they could have seen some improvement. It wasn't like a real ritzy area, it wasn't the Taj Mahal—it was a working person's area." Because our speakers were aware of the "blight" designation used by city elites to justify the demolition of their part of town, they often spoke vociferously against it, as we have seen (chapter 2). Many of the families in this area owned their own homes, however small. This was especially the case with long-standing Lebanese and Italian families, many of whom operated small shops such as bakeries or grocery stores on the bottom floor. Many black families were long-standing homeowners as well, as we address shortly. But those without independent businesses often worked at local factories, including steel mills, silk mills, and garment factories. And all admitted that their families struggled.

Poverty emerged as an important theme in Larry's reminiscences. During another lengthy monologue, he discussed how his family used to buy live chickens from a neighbor down the street, adding that they ate a lot of chicken and a lot of macaroni. His wife, Dot, interrupted, perhaps to explain the point of his discussion to the younger woman interviewing them:

LARRY: We had lots of macaroni and lots of chicken.

DOT: They were poor.

LARRY: Oh yeah, we were very poor. We didn't—our area, the area down in that area, which is now a nice area, it, it was uh a fairly poor section. We didn't have sewers in that area until the fifties, the 1950s. We had an outhouse until the 1950s. We didn't have central heat until the . . . [long pause while calculating years] Oh, I went into the service in 1956, and I think it was around that time that we got central heat. We used to have a coal stove in the kitchen!

Larry's father died when he was two, and he grew up with a stepsister, his mother, and his grandmother. He explained, "So I was the only man in the house. And I had to take care of everything, you know, like, so, I grew up very young." Pam had a similar story: her mother left the family when she was thirteen: "And my mother left, and my father raised us, and I was the lady of the house at thirteen, and I had to cook, clean, take care of my brothers, while my father worked." A central point in her interview was her insistence on staying in school while it was expected that she would leave school to work in the factories like all of her peers.

Poverty also came up when former residents were talking together in smaller group settings, as during regular meetings of the elementary school organizing committee. One woman laughed remembering the elementary school photographer commenting on her wearing the same dress every year for her school portrait. Two men reminisced about how they would make their own football out of newspaper and string.

Men talked about putting cardboard in their shoes for insulation in the winter, and all remembered the long hours their parents worked. During a discussion with Dorothy and her daughter Cindy, Cindy prompted her mother to talk about the Great Depression. Dorothy replied, "No, they didn't lose anything [during the Depression] because they didn't really *have* anything to lose. Our people did not get hurt by the Depression." These patterns shed light on an alternative mode of differentiation being asserted, one rooted in class, which was inscribed in the cityscape. People's reminiscences were imbued with an understanding that their neighborhood's ethnic diversity was deeply tied to its place in a wider class hierarchy, one that situated them in an inferior status to people living elsewhere.

In this regard, it is useful to consider "adequation" and "distinction," two "tactics of intersubjectivity" proposed by Bucholtz and Hall.[30] Adequation, the "pursuit of socially recognized sameness," can help construct unity, however temporary, while distinction is a mechanism "whereby salient difference is produced."[31] We can see the process of adequation at work in the lumping together of individuals of different citizenship statuses with the truncated ethnonyms ("Lebanese," etc.). We also believe that adequation results from the vernacular use of "nationality," which allows "blacks," "Jews," "Lebanese," and "Italians" to be considered equivalent types of people.

Distinction is at work in these narratives as well. In his work on memories of the Argentine Chaco, Gastón Gordillo demonstrates that understandings of a place are perpetually constituted and reconstituted in relation to other places.[32] Similarly, Syrian Town was understood in contrast to other locales. Alongside the explicit narrative of diversity in Syrian Town, our interviewees told a story of a deeper class hierarchy dividing the city. Their stories of poverty become more meaningful in the context of the wider city geography and social relations. They especially distinguished their "ethnic" neighborhood culturally and economically from the wealthy, "nonethnic" College Hill, a neighborhood located on a steep hill overlooking the downtown area that was the long-standing home of the city elite. Deixis becomes the key to understanding the way these divisions are communicated in their stories. We could argue that when former residents talked together about Syrian Town, they operated from a shared "deictic center." In her work on Mount Pleasant, a neighborhood of Washington, DC, Gabriella Modan defines a "deictic center" as a "base point where a speaker locates themselves spatially, temporally, and socially." She considers the rhetorical strategies used in a grant proposal to "set up a rigid distinction between core and marginal members of the community."[33] In the Syrian Town story world, it was clear that the "we" in the narratives were residents of Syrian Town, who were often opposed to a more distant, abstract "they" located spatially in College Hill. Note the way Anthony, the older Lebanese man who had tried to prevent renewal, outlines the villains of his story. Over the course of a long monologue in which the octogenarian discussed his memories of the renewal era, he said, "The powers that be that were in power . . . *they*'d destroy any foreign neighborhood. *They* looked down on nationalities." It is implied here that the "they" in question were of an unmarked ethnic background, since they "looked down on nationalities."

We find a similar shadowy distant population in our interview with Gloria. We asked if the neighborhood also had people of German background:

ALS: Were there any of German background, like Pennsylvania Dutch families?

GLORIA: Well, if there was, it wasn't that many that I . . . [*trails off*]

ALS: At your school?

GLORIA: Oh, the Lebanese, the Italians, and the blacks would overrun any of that. And I guess because there was *all those ethnic groups* at Taylor School, that maybe there were *some people* who looked *down upon* that, you know? Wouldn't want their kids to go to that school. I think that was the attitude of some people.

Gloria doesn't identify who "some people" are, but we sense their distance from her: they were looking *down on* her. In another conversation, she told us she imagined that local elites viewed the neighborhood as "all those ethnic peoples *down* there." In both cases, Gloria is imagining people living above her, indexing in a parsimonious fashion both higher class status and an elevated physical location. She imagines this unnamed population considering neighborhood residents as "those ethnic groups," and thus we can infer that "they" are of unmarked ethnicity. Sometimes this elevated location is spelled out directly. In another part of the conversation, we discussed whether or not everyone's stories of yesteryear would be the same. Gloria replied quickly, "Let me tell you this: if you interviewed someone who lived on College Hill, you would get a different opinion of what I've just told you. College Hill people kind of look *down upon* Lehigh Street." She went on to add, "It was a really nice place to grow up, nice area to grow up. 'Cause you got the *mixture*. Maybe if today people could understand one another's . . . *ethnic people*, maybe it'd be a nicer life, a nicer world." We see here the "mixture" and "ethnic people" contrasted with a College Hill perspective on the neighborhood.

In another part of our interview, Gloria told a story about a specific resident from College Hill, her landlord, coming by chauffeured car to collect the rent:

> GLORIA: I can't remember the name of the man that owned them [talking about the little houses she and her extended family lived in], but I can picture him coming, not really a limousine, but a nice big car, chauffeur driven, and he'd collect the rent from everybody.
> AE: Wow, huh!
> ALS: It's really interesting. Yeah, I wonder who it was.
> GLORIA: I don't know. He was from College Hill, 'cause College Hill was where all the um . . . the dignitaries or whatever . . . [*trails off*].

In these conversations with Gloria, all participants would be classified as "white," although Gloria is uncomfortable with such a label, as we discuss shortly. College Hill appears in even sharper contrast in the following conversations involving black interlocutors. In the first instance, Mark and Edna, two black former residents, are speaking with a young white female student. Mark is explaining that for kids in the Taylor School district, the kids in neighboring West Easton, the next elementary school district, were "off limits":

MARK: The kids who lived up on 9th, 10th Streets, those kids were off limits. They had their place up there, and we had our place down here. College Hill? Forget it!

EDNA: Oh yeah, they were snooty!

STUDENT: Yeah, that's what we've heard. It still kind of has that feel.

MARK: Yeah, well, most of the people who lived up there were wealthy.

EDNA: They were wealthy. That was considered wealthy up there. It was like the rich cream of the crop. People who lived up there were lawyers and doctors.

The conversation was even more pointed when a black student interviewed Mark and his long-lost buddy, Don, of Italian descent, whom he hadn't seen in years. Mark liked to challenge people's memories, and he did so at first with Don; the conversation again leads into a distinction made between their neighborhood and College Hill:

MARK: Where did we go swimming, do you remember?

DON: Wilson Dam!

MARK (TO STUDENT): We would call it B-A-B, Bare Ass Beach. We couldn't go on the other side—that was the College Hill gang. They stayed up there, and we stayed down here.

DON (AGAIN, TO STUDENT): College Hill was the affluent place of the city—big homes—they're still up there. Doctors, lawyers, businessmen. Very influential people who had big businesses in Easton live up there now. There was discrimination, let me tell you.

MARK: At that time, we couldn't go up there, us black people, you couldn't afford to go up there. My mother, she used to go up there and clean for somebody.

We can see in these discussions the construction of a deictic center that includes the neighborhood and its residents and an imagined peripheral location and people described as elites located "above" who looked "down upon" Syrian Town. Ethnic diversity is linked to class standing and distinguishes Syrian Town from the unmarked, "nonethnic," elite neighborhood to the north. Even Syrian Town's microsegregation was viewed as nominal in comparison to the segregation dividing the city as a whole. When we asked if there was hidden segregation in Easton, looking for information on the block-level segregation in Syrian Town, Jerry misunderstood and replied, "Yes, the only black people up on College Hill were the domestics. They went up on College Hill to cook for them, took care of their kids, but couldn't live up there." This was distinction of a different scale.

Ethnic labels directly indexed common membership in the same neighborhood and indirectly indexed social class.[34] Rather than participating in a covert "racialization," as we see in Stanton Wortham and colleagues' discussion of ethnic mentions, we find "class-ification."[35] Ethnic labels help to describe a certain kind of place populated by a certain kind of people and become virtually obligatory for the former neighborhood residents, for whom they served as a covert membership card. Claiming one of Syrian Town's ethnic labels (as in "I'm Lebanese") could be viewed as taking a particular stance.[36] In this case, it was an authentic connection to the former neighborhood. Because the neighborhood's residents, as "ethnics," were understood to be poor relative to the rest of the city, the ethnic labels indirectly index a working-class background, calling to mind a deeper division mapped onto the city's very landscape.

The Exception That Proves the Rule

Embedded within these narratives are details suggesting a specific construction of whiteness associated with College Hill. As a usually unmarked term, "white" stands "opposite and unequal" to surrounding terms and takes "its meaning from those surrounding categories to which it is structurally opposed."[37] In contrast to the diverse, ethnic Syrian Town, College Hill is nonethnic, rich, and elite. We can infer that the prevailing "tropes of whiteness" associated with this opposing neighborhood, from the perspective of our speakers, were "white as privileged upper class," "white as elite."[38] We see this with Gloria's description of her landlord being driven down to collect his rent because he was one of the "dignitaries" and Anthony's discussion of an elite group that "looked down on nationalities." For Lakhota narrators in Sara Trechter's study, whiteness "is sometimes presupposed in conversations for strategic purposes." As Trechter writes, "Speakers create a dialogue with whiteness, foregrounding and indexing its individualistic character as they negotiate their positions in and around Lakhota culture."[39] In our case, we find whiteness indexing class and location in the wider cityscape and associated with "snootiness." Syrian Town residents defined themselves in clear opposition to this largely unmarked, white population.

The association between neighborhood residence, ethnic labeling, and working-class status became problematic for Gloria, a woman of German English ancestry, at least on one occasion when we queried her directly on how she would identify herself. She had married a Sicilian man and talked to us about having mostly Italian and Lebanese friends growing up. During the end of our interview, we finally interrupted to ask how she would describe herself:

ALS: And when you were talking about everybody, the Italians and the Lebanese, how would you define yourself when you were that age? Would you say you were American? Or? [*pause*]

AE: That's a question I had too.

GLORIA: Know what? I never gave it a thought! I guess I would say I'm an American, but I don't think I ever . . . [*trails off*]

ALS: Would they call you English or something?

GLORIA: I don't know what they would call me!

While her hedging may be representative of the difficulty white people have in seeing their whiteness,[40] it seemed to us that it also underscored her confusion at confronting her own lack of a suitable ethnic label. At the same time, she didn't elicit the label "white" for herself. We wondered if local class-linked understandings of whiteness, a whiteness associated with "snootiness" and "dignitaries," prevented her from placing herself in that category.

Breaking the Chain of Indexicality

Gabriella Modan's work reveals an entire web of indexicality operating in the Mount Pleasant community.[41] She notes that community members discuss the city and suburb through a set of ideological contrasts such as heterogeneous versus homogeneous, disorderly versus orderly, dangerous versus safe, allowing "social actors to use any of these characteristics to index any of the others, or to index urban or suburban identity." In this way, "whiteness can be used to index fear, fear can be used to index gender . . . and any of these can be—and are—used by community members to index a suburban identity that is juxtaposed to the city," which is in turn associated with filth, noise, masculinity, and so forth.[42]

Similarly, in Easton, "blight" was associated locally with "slum," which in turn was closely associated with black people, as we have seen. Through this indexical chain, "blight" and "slum" are code words for race. The association of African Americans with blight emerged by the beginning of the twentieth century on a national scale, as real estate agents, brokers, and mortgage bankers believed that blacks' presence would undermine property values and lead to deterioration.[43] Rather than trying to identify neighborhoods where the buildings were in need of repair, realtors and bankers created a shortcut, seemingly finding it easier to count the number of "minorities" in a given location; as Kevin Gotham writes, "Builders and developers and appraisal firms also analyzed racial migration trends."[44] One could argue that they were mistaking a relationship of correlation with causation. Taken up by federal agencies, racially discriminatory policies such as redlining were developed in which mixed or black-majority neighborhoods automatically received less funding, setting into play an open racial discrimination that would have longstanding consequences. To identify poor neighborhoods, officials just had to look for black people rather than decaying structures.

In the case of Syrian Town, this logic did not hold. Here, the majority of the structures were in decent shape, and this was also where most black people lived in the city. In fact, many of the black families we interviewed or that people talked about were homeowners before demolition began; as Agatha reported, "The Afro-Americans that lived next door, I got <u>news</u> for you, they had a home out of this world! [She discusses their children's occupations.] They were like high class!" In discussing the neighborhood at their reunions and in our interviews, our interlocutors seemed to be challenging the dominant indexical chain and instead asserting what Jan Blommaert has termed "local indexicality."[45] *We were different*, their narratives tell us. *Blacks lived here, among others, and we were not living in slums; we were not blighted.* Their insistence that Syrian Town had been composed of distinct "nationalities" (and not just so-called Syrians) and their downplaying of racializing language could be viewed in the same light. We might also see their engagement with processes of "adequation" in stories of ethnic harmony as part of a wider challenge to the dominant indexical chain of associations, associations that had led to real material consequences for their neighborhood.

Concluding Remarks

Much of the scholarship on the emergence of a black/white racial binary has developed (with good reason) from empirical studies of more racially polarized American cities and often from macrolevel analyses that can obscure the complexities of people's ways of identifying themselves and others. In his landmark work on racial inequality in postwar Detroit, for instance, Thomas Sugrue argues that the principal cleavages in the city were racial ones, and he describes the history of residential, occupational, and educational segregation that polarized the city and involved so many violent conflicts. Although the city's white population was ethnically quite diverse, he deemphasizes ethnicity, writing that "by the 1920s, the city's tightly knit ethnic clusters had begun to disperse," and a "dwindling number of Detroit residents found themselves living in communities defined by ethnicity." As a result, he adds, "residents of Detroit's white neighborhoods abandoned their ethnic affiliations and found a new identity in their whiteness."[46] In his study of the neighborhood associations that proliferated after 1943, his archival sources "seldom referred to national heritage or religious background"; instead, he found that ethnic nomenclature was reserved for "the colored," "Asians," or "Jews." Neighborhood and homeowners groups "shared a common bond of whiteness and Americanness," referring to themselves as the "white race."[47] While studies based on other cities may fine-tune the timing of the emergence of a consolidated white identity,[48] most works leave the racializing trajectory, and especially the eventual evolution of a white identity, in place.

The speaking patterns of our elderly interviewees challenge these trends. Not only were *ethnic* labels relevant in the 1960s (and continue to be so today), but we also encountered very little racial "binary-making" language and rarely heard the term "white." It appears that the Italians and Lebanese living in this particular part of town were not actively involved in claiming a white racial identity, as Sugrue found in Detroit. The more important distinctions fell along class, not racial, lines.

A study of ethnonymic systems yields insights into local understandings of the social world. In the present example, this method has allowed us to develop a "folk" or vernacular approach to race and ethnicity prominent in the 1960s in one neighborhood of a small city, a folk model that does not exactly map onto standard academic definitions. People in this neighborhood saw each other as members of distinct nationalities, which in the local vernacular was an unproblematic quality tied to an individual's ancestry and denoted by a liberal use of ethnonyms. Nationality, like race and ethnicity in other settings, can function as a "strategically deployable shifter."[49] At the same time, interviewees talked about each other as members of a single community that stood in opposition to the elites of College Hill. Ethnonyms in this neighborhood were thus obligatory markers not only of ethnic distinctions but also of an unstated class status. The deeper and more significant social division in this town, from the point of view of our speakers, was between the "ethnic people" and the unmarked (white) elites living "above" them. The ethnonymic labeling of the social world, then, alerts us to a covert construction of whiteness, a whiteness indicative of wealth, power, and privilege and devoid of ethnic attachments. By indirectly indexing this unmarked, covert construction of whiteness, ethnonyms helped to communicate the fusion of ethnic diversity, class, and place in a city that, at least until renewal struck the heart of the town, was most sharply divided along these lines. These statements carried with them an implicit judgment about the contemporary social order, an order that is the direct result of the processes that destroyed Syrian Town.

As we shall see later in this book, the demolition of Syrian Town drastically accelerated processes of segregation, and most of the former residents have spent the past half-century in racially homogeneous neighborhoods. Thus, contemporary circumstances make the narratives "tellable" in that they describe a situation that is comparatively rare today and worth noting. The ethnic labels we heard did something more, too: in many cases, old-fashioned labels lent an old-timey feel to the narratives and seemed to promote further stories of the lost neighborhood in the past. As such, these labels did more than help describe a whole social world in all its complexity, they were also key catalysts in the processes of remembering. The ways language, place, and time were mutually reinforcing features that shaped the ways the former residents talked with each other at their parties and reunions are the focus of our next chapter.

4. Voices from the Past

At the start of our first reunion, Jerry was looking at a map of Syrian Town. As Anna introduced herself, Jerry pointed out key neighborhood features to her, leading to a somewhat confused interaction:

JERRY: So 6th and Northampton. That was an area of ill repute.
AE: It was?
JERRY: Area of ill repute.
AE: How come?
JERRY: They had white slavery there. They used to come across the bridge.
AE: Mhmmm.
JERRY: If you went two blocks, that's where the two-dollar bill is called "upstairs money."
AE: Huh. Wow.
JERRY: [*chuckles*] In fact, if you was to go up to [discusses the tearing down of buildings to create a parking lot]. They tore down all those houses.
AE: Yeah, but you said there was slavery there?
JERRY: White slavery they called it. Prostitutes.
AE: *Oh.* OK.

"Ill repute." "White slavery." "Upstairs money." "6th and Northampton." Phrases like these stuck out in our field notes following early encounters like this one. Our speakers knew we were interested in life in Syrian Town and thus mostly talked to us about that time and place. We heard stories of ethnic harmony, of a neighborhood so safe that people "never locked their doors." We listened to tales of childhood antics:

playing on rooftops, sliding down an icy hill on the way to school, and playing football. We heard of family life: the grandparents who ran a store downstairs or who lived on the next block and watched the children while the mothers worked in the local garment factories. In the process of talking to us, our speakers often used terms from a past era that jarred us at first or that took effort to translate, as we see in the conversation that opens this chapter, where Anna had trouble understanding "white slavery," finally translated as "prostitution."

Outdated terms like this abound in stories of Syrian Town. Many are associated with fashions, practices, or occupations of yesteryear, such as "ice man," "bar room," "coal man," and "slouch hat." Over the course of our research with this community, we began to refer to these words and phrases as "past terms" and the practice of using them as "past talk." The ethnic labels that are out of fashion today (e.g., "Afro-American," which we elucidate in the previous chapter) can also be viewed as "past terms." By engaging these distinctive "processes of identification" in their narratives, our speakers relay a specific understanding of the social world no longer operative in the contemporary era.[1] Because labels for several of the ethnic categories changed rapidly (e.g., Negro to Afro-American and black, or Syrian to Lebanese), the "pastness" of these labels is especially apparent. Finally, people loved to share former place-names: names of streets and alleys that are no longer part of the cityscape; names of specific locations, such as the ice house; or names of specific shops, such as the Zingales Italian Grocery and Thatcher's Fish Market. These evocations of the geography of the former neighborhood were sometimes the most widely shared and repeated, as we discuss below.

"Past talk" elucidates a well-known Bakhtinian concept. In his essay, "Discourse in the Novel," Russian philosopher and literary critic Mikhail Bakhtin coined the term "heteroglossia" to refer to the "simultaneous use of different kinds of speech."[2] These different kinds of speech result from the constant evolution of language. Various "stratifying factors"— age group, socioeconomic position, and geographical area—mean that even the "same" language varies considerably over social space.[3]

Scholars have found the notion of heteroglossia, now the topic of a vast literature across linguistic and cultural anthropology, productive for exploring the poetics and politics of language choice in multilingual situations. The concept has enriched our understanding of the interaction of multiple registers and the use by one individual of a "kaleidoscope" of voices within a storytelling session. As we invoke the concept here, we focus on the *temporal* dimensions of the instances of heteroglossia we have uncovered. Instead of focusing on the interaction of different ways of speaking located in one place and time (e.g., the talk of contemporary car salesmen and that of lawyers from the same time and place), we wish to emphasize a shifting back and forth between temporal realms, what we refer to as "temporal heteroglossia."[4] We use this appellation to single out a particular heteroglossic feature of our informants' speech that is instrumental in their relationship to their past and to each other.

Bakhtin himself emphasized temporality in his original explication of heteroglossia: "Each generation at each social level has its own language; moreover, every age group has as a matter of fact its own language, its own vocabulary, its own particular accentual system." In turn, "at any given moment, languages of various epochs and periods of socio-ideological life cohabit with one another" and are thus in dialogue.[5] As language evolves, words from the past come into dialogue with contemporary ways of speaking. And as language evolves, the very old among us will have lived through slow but constant shifts in the language practices of the social groups of which they are a part and should have at their disposal a whole array of ways of speaking rooted in different eras, reflecting their whole "language biography."[6] People do not necessarily forget former ways of speaking but may instead slip back and forth between different historical variations in language over the course of a single conversation. We have identified a rich set of such confrontations as voices of the past erupt in the speech of today, a form of heteroglossia that is decidedly "temporal" in nature.

Because language is inherently infused and interanimated with others' voices, distinguishing a language of "today" and that of "yesterday" could seem a fool's errand. As Judith Irvine writes, "A temporality . . . is built into discursive practice."[7] However, the unique circumstances of our study, which involves people who talk about a place and time eradicated fifty years ago and who have not seen each other since, may have encouraged this past talk, this language of yesterday, to surface. The fact that this has been a collaborative project involving considerably younger student researchers has also helped, for it made what we might consider past terms more noticeable. Given the considerable historical and social distance from the present that animates Syrian Town narratives, it is perhaps no surprise that the narratives we have heard are rich in temporal heteroglossia. Attending to this mechanism in descriptions of the past carries important implications for understanding historical narratives, and this concept helps advance an anthropology of history, as we develop below.

Lost Places, Evocative Objects, and Verbal Relics

At Taylor School reunions, conversations centered on the neighborhood itself: its streets and structures. Hours of our recorded interviews are descriptive: people walked us through the neighborhood, recounting it building by building. We heard about persisting material proof of the neighborhood's existence. One person told us about mint plants that still come up where his former home once stood. Another invited us to go on a tour of the city so that he could show us the surviving signs of the city before urban renewal, such as locations where the sidewalk changes color. These details seem small, but they are reassuring pieces of evidence of the residents' past.

As archaeologist Julia Hendon explains, physical settings perform a semiotic function in the work of memory, reminding people of the way it felt to be part of that setting.[8] In this sense, place can serve as a key "framework" for collective remembering, as others have noted.[9] But what happens when the place itself no longer exists? When the built environment no longer stands, how do people engage with it through memory?

In semiotic terms, we could view artifacts of Syrian Town as "signs of history." "Signs of" and "signs in history" are concepts developed by Richard Parmentier in his study of the Belau of Western Micronesia to elucidate signs used in Belauan history. "Signs of history" are "representational expressions which, through iconic, indexical, and residually symbolic properties, record and classify events as history." They often come from the spatiotemporal contexts of the events to which they refer. An example would be a pen used in signing a key document, or remnants of George Washington's house. These items often carry with them an "aura" derived from their presumed contiguity with the original context, and for this reason they may be preserved and protected. In and of themselves, these objects don't necessarily describe what happened; this is the function of "signs in history," signs that offer some "intentional description or categorization of what kinds of events, actions, or processes are at issue," such as an "epic poem depicting events from another era, or a commemorative postage stamp," or, in our case, stories about Syrian Town. In his work, Parmentier is interested in how in many oral societies, "signs of history" are often at the same time "signs in history."[10] In the next chapter, we will discuss further the power of various seemingly insignificant physical objects for our speakers and their quality as "signs of history." Here, we want to argue that elements of speech, what we might see as "linguistic artifacts," can serve as "signs of history" as well.[11]

Specific terms from the past circulate, helping not only to comment on the past world but also to rebuild it: as we show, by talking about the former place and time, the Syrian Town chronotope itself generates past terms and elicits further storytelling. Past terms, then, are both descriptive and highly productive. Given the absence of physical remains, language that had been used in the old neighborhood—now outdated—seems to have become especially significant. Reunion gatherings provided former residents with a unique venue in which to talk about neighborhood memories together, sharing what remained of the vanished place, remains that took form not only in the old photographs and colored sidewalks but also in the use of particular ways of speaking. We now turn to explore the quality of language as artifact in stories about Syrian Town.

Tale Telling, Time Traveling, and Temporal Heteroglossia

As speakers describe life in Syrian Town, they recall that place during a particular time, the years before demolition. We could say that their stories relate to a particular place-in-time, or "chronotope" (literally, "time-space"). Chronotope is another Bakhtinian neologism originally applied to the mutual constitution of temporality and place in the novel form.[12] Linguistic anthropologists have usefully elaborated on this idea: Michael Silverstein defines chronotope as "the temporally (hence, *chrono-*)

and spatially (hence, -*tope*) particular envelope in the narrated universe of social space-time in which and through which, in emplotment, narrative characters move."[13] Asif Agha stresses the fusing of place and time with a certain type of personhood, showing that a given chronotope is peopled by particular social types.[14] Others explore how speakers may strategically "telescope" time, bringing the past into the present by indexing different chronotopes in their speech.[15] This is often observed in religious ritual, in which the very pastness of the voices grants them special moral authority.[16] In contrast to many of the other works of linguistic anthropology utilizing the chronotope framework, however, our speakers were not *necessarily* selecting words that carried any special authority due to their pastness, as we develop later.

Sabina Perrino notes that personal narratives are expected to be in the past "by default," and speakers use various linguistic resources (such as past tense) to ensure that the event being narrated is not confused with the present storytelling event; as a result, the two events are "made to occupy separate 'chronotopes.'"[17] In this regard, personal narratives will always involve a kind of "cross-chronotope time travel" in that speakers will lead listeners to a former place-in-time. Our speakers invoke the Syrian Town chronotope not only through past tense or metapragmatic framing devices such as the phrase "back then" but also through certain outdated nouns.[18] This recalls Charles Briggs's Córdovan informants, who employ a set of expressions he terms "multiplex signs" (like references to goats and sheep, threshing, moccasins, and hard work), the pragmatic force of which reminds people of bygone days; these expressions stand "as abbreviations for the chain of events that deprived Córdovans of the self-sufficiency that they had enjoyed for nearly two hundred years."[19] As Syrian Town residents "time travel" across chronotopes, their utterance is peppered with striking past words as they engage in "temporal heteroglossia." Temporal heteroglossia as analytic enables us to unpack the various ways in which speakers' use of past terms is significant to their stories and to advance the way we understand language's role in the work of memory.

We now turn to three different ways past terms emerged in our interlocutors' speech: when they cite voices from the past, when they are "accidentally" motivated by the story world itself, and when they use place-names.

Others' Words

"Syrian" was a term from the past that often emerged in our speakers' stories. This ethnonym shifted to "Lebanese" after World War II, and our speakers were well aware that community members at some point preferred the label "Lebanese." In discussing the present day, speakers invariably employed the Lebanese ethnonym. However, they often shifted to Syrian when discussing their memories of the distant past; this occurred especially in reported speech.

Anthony, the Lebanese man who had fought the renewal project, had strong words against anti-Lebanese sentiment, as we have seen. We return to his statement to now consider use of labels: "The powers that be that were in power, they'd destroy any foreign neighborhood They looked down on nationalities. Now, believe me, they know who you are, what nationality you are. Inside, a lot of them haven't gotten over that, you know what I'm talking about? They'll be nice to you and all that, but 'He's a *Syrian*,' and that happens to all nationalities. They think the Lebanese are all moonshine peddlers. Some of them never get it out of their heads." We see here Anthony using the dated "Syrian" label in his reported speech in a way that suggests he is ventriloquizing a xenophobe in his story ("They'll be nice to you and all that, but 'He's a *Syrian*'").

Another interesting example occurred when we were talking with a woman in her eighties, Dorothy, and her daughter in her sixties, Cindy. Over the course of the taped conversation, they began to discuss the "Syrian" label outright:

> CINDY: They didn't call us "Lebanese." They called us "Syrian." They used to say this was a "Syrian Town," "Going on down to the *Syrian* Town," but we weren't *Syrians*.
>
> DOROTHY: Yeah, they used to call us *Syrian* Town. We're not *Syrians*. We are *Lebanese*. Even the nun in school, I got her in trouble for that. We were Catholic girls. We went to the Catholic school. Like, you know, when you'd get in uhhh . . . an assembly with the other girls, we was talking and we was

joking. The nun was trying to have an assembly to practice singing, and me and my friends were sitting back there. We weren't the only Lebanese girls, but there were other Irish girls sitting back there with us, talking. We weren't talking loud. We were talking and joking. "What are you doing back there, you dumb <u>Syrians</u>! We couldn't teach your parents anything. Well, I guess we're not going to teach *you* anything!" And we slumped down into the seats. We went home crying that day. And boy, did she get it.

There are several interesting features of this coconstructed story. When talking about themselves in the past, the women deploy "Lebanese" ("We weren't the only Lebanese girls"). In this case, they use a contemporary term to discuss a past time (see chapter 3 for a history of labels for immigrants from Lebanon and their descendants). And yet, in approximating the nun's tirade, Dorothy shifts to "Syrian," which, as in Anthony's case, seems to exemplify non-Lebanese ignorance. The case of parodying an out-group by imagining its members employing dated language is an interesting example of temporal heteroglossia that suggests that ethnic labels, which may shift rapidly and may be politically charged, can be important past terms that serve as verbal resources allowing speakers to position themselves as "forward-thinking," as insiders, and to position others as bigots. By using past terms in reanimating others' speech, speakers make a claim about their own progressive social values.

In using another's speech for the speaker's own purposes (or "double voicing"), speakers can re-create various ways of speaking. In Jane Hill's essay on voicing, she shows how her interlocutor, Don Gabriel, constructs a system of at least twenty voices through which he tells the narrative of his son's death, imbuing specific episodes, characters, and spaces of the story with particular moral valences.[20] Much work on reported speech suggests that it functions "not to replicate actual utterances but to create utterances typical of culturally specific types of *personas.*"[21] Scholars may question why speakers inhabit or ventriloquize these personas in particular and have found that reported speech allows the speaker to play the role of both animator (in Erving Goffman's terms, the person who utters a set of words) and author (the individual to whom the words are attributed).[22] In this way, speakers can take varying stances toward the different personae developed in their narrations or the topics under discussion.[23] While this certainly holds true in the Syrian Town narrative above, at the same time we would like to point out the impossibility of using anything *but* this past term to communicate this scene.

It appears that in Dorothy's narration of speech from a past era, a contemporary term just wouldn't do. We may never know if the nun in question said these exact words or if this phrasing was the result of Dorothy performing an imaginary persona, such as "the racist" or "the ignorant outsider." But we can also argue that the "Syrian" label in the reported speech of the nun represented a more authentic or plausible-sounding former way of speaking. Indeed, if Dorothy had narrated this story, which dated to a time (the 1930s) before the creation of the state of Lebanon (1946), using the label "Lebanese" instead, it would have sounded untrue to listeners of the speaker's age group.

Past Terms Generated by the Story World

A second kind of utterance that yielded past terms has quite a different flavor to us. It seemed that it was the *content* of the stories narrated that generated past terms over the course of a narration as if they emerged from the story world.[24] We consider them chronotope-generated past terms. Here we focus on outdated terms such as "nationality" and antiquated colloquial expressions such as "the cat's meow."

"Nationality" came up frequently, and it took some work to fully understand, as we have discussed in the previous chapter. We have seen it already in Anthony's long passage cited earlier.

Rather than referring to different groups within the neighborhood as "ethnic groups," interlocutors typically called them "nationalities." They used the term "nationalities" to refer to both ethnic and racial groups. What we find most significant is the fact that "nationality," along with the distinctive ethnic labeling system we have been discussing, occurred in speakers' stories regardless of the phrases that we, Anna and Andrea, used. When we asked about "Lebanese Americans," people simply referred to "Lebanese." When we asked about the different "ethnic groups" in the neighborhood, people consistently responded as Pam, Jerry, and Anthony did by talking about the "nationalities."

"Syrian" emerged in this way as well. While Anthony and Susan seemed to strategically select "Syrian" in narrating the speech of xenophobes, this term also appeared in other stories, prompted, it seems to us, by the very act of narrating a former time. The case of the African American woman Rosie is especially interesting, for she used both labels. In a taped discussion (following our use of "Lebanese" to refer to the old neighborhood), she explained, "When I'd be like six and seven, I'd be sitting down there with the Lebanese ladies in black . . . all the widows, you know?" However, later on in the interview, she told a story to illustrate how neighborhood residents looked out for each other regardless of ethnic background: "So I went to get a license, and the old Syrian guy that was down at city hall, you know, he was asking, he said 'Do you know James and Harry?' and I says, 'Yeah, that's my dad and my uncle.'" It appears that in imagining herself walking into city hall that day, she slipped into the older Syrian label to narrate her story.

We found a similar deployment of varying labels for blacks. As noted, labels for African Americans are the subject of a wide and important literature.[25] (Labels have ranged from African and free versus slave to colored, Negro, black, and African American.) As particular labels became charged with negative associations, black leaders promoted new ones.[26] The promotion and adoption of new labels, however, have not always corresponded with a systematic extinction of old terms (often to the dismay of activists), and overlapping terminology may persist despite the shifts in ideas that such terms index.

Over the course of our interviews, many interviewees slipped into older labels for African Americans such as colored and Afro-American. Dorothy described microlevel segregation as follows: "West Street was mostly *colored* people, but they didn't bother us. We grew up with them." By "colored," she did not mean the class of people associated with that term as it is used today, such as in South Africa. Her memory of West Street seemed linked with the word "colored," a term used while she was living in the neighborhood. Similarly, during the long interview in which Agatha discussed the people who lived on her old street, she explained, "The *Afro-Americans* that lived next door, I got news for you, they had a home that was out of this world." To her, they were Afro-Americans as the term had designated them in the past.

A former teacher from the neighborhood elementary school, Daniel, resorted to several dated expressions during his narration of personal experiences. When we spoke with him, he voiced his awareness of the erroneous nature of the Syrian label; regarding the neighborhood, he said, "Everybody said that's where the *Syrians* lived. That's how we knew it as. Never said *Lebanese*, it was always *Syrians*." Nevertheless, he used the term later in the same discussion: "I had some trepidations. They were *Syrians*, I was an eight- or nine-year-old kid. I was raised in the German community, and I knew they weren't Germans. When I would go into the area with my dad, my eyes got big like Orphan Annie's!" We should note not only his use of Syrian but also his reference to Orphan Annie, a dated popular figure. This passage suggests that he was traveling back in time in his mind, returning to see the world through child's eyes as he remembered what it felt like to go to the neighborhood in those early years.

A similar shift into the language of the time occurred when seventy-nine-year-old Martha was discussing a typical outing with her future husband in a longer discussion of how they were happy with so little: "On a Sunday afternoon, when I was dating my husband, he would take me to Jack's Hot Dogs or somewhere for a milkshake and a ride. Well, that was the cat's meow." Following a significant pause, she asked, "You know that expression? The cat's meow?" Again, it appeared that phrases such as "Orphan Annie" and "the cat's meow" emerged in the context of the storytelling itself.

Place-Names as Past Terms

The abundant place-names that we heard in all conversations about the past are also past terms, for they denote dated structures that no longer exist. Large portions of our meetings were spent discussing former stores and vanished pieces of the cityscape. It was as if the participants in our project took great pleasure in repeating this litany of place-names, describing the vanished streets and sites of many of their childhood antics. While we assiduously typed up stories about the ways of yesteryear—the rag man who would drive a horse and wagon yelling "I'll buy," or the mules that pulled the ice wagons—we sometimes neglected to retype the old shop names that fill our handwritten field notes: the Shed House, Henry's, Shop 'N Stop, Sun Carpet, Howard's Motors. At first they didn't seem important to us, but, as we soon learned, the names of places, stores, and shops were sometimes the focus of whole conversations and often were recited back and forth in rapid fashion, as in the following example:

"Easton on Friday night was packed! You couldn't walk on the sidewalk but had to walk in the street!"
"Do you remember all the department stores we had?"
"Oh yeah, there was Woolworth's!"
"Grant's!"
"Kresge's!"
"Woolworth's!"
"And all the movie theaters."
"My mom would pack a lunch, and we'd watch those movies a couple times!"
"The Ranch House used to cost fifteen cents!"
"Remember the Berwick?"
"What about the State Theatre?"
"We used to sneak in the back door."
"Don't forget the Boyd Theatre—it was called the Seville after that."

During an early reunion, a group of men that included a pair of octogenarian childhood friends and several newcomers all spoke at once. It was difficult to capture in our notes the enthusiasm or the specific places they shouted back and forth to each other. Hours of our recorded individual interviews are descriptive as well: people walked us through the neighborhood, recounting it building by building. People often located their stories precisely in the city's former geography, and they identified each other in this way as well. During the first elementary school reunion we had, when men and women meeting for the first time decided to go around the room to introduce themselves, three pieces of information were necessary: the years they attended the school, their names (and maiden name for married women), and the street they lived on. Often the surname was enough, and listeners filled in the street name, leading to laughter or even applause. In many ways, it appeared that narrating place-name past terms was a necessary feature of fitting a newcomer into the reunion then under way. We will consider the implications of these observations for an understanding of the relationship of materiality and memory in the next chapter. For now, we want to consider what these cases of temporal heteroglossia tell us about storytelling, memory, and language.

Chronotopes as Generative, as "Instigators"

Metanarrative about words and their meanings indicates that speakers sometimes were carried away by their very stories only to realize that the words they were using to tell them were out-of-date. Analysis of narrative in linguistic anthropology typically celebrates the performative and poetic genius of interlocutors' storytelling and often carries explicit or implicit assumptions about speaker agency and intentionality. Given the politics of conducting social science research in general and that of representation specifically, it is difficult to argue the reverse. And yet, in our second category of temporal heteroglossia, the past terms seemed to emerge as if by accident. Speakers did not *always* seem to be selecting these phrases strategically to make a point; rather, they slipped into the past way of talking automatically as they were remembering the place-in-time. These examples suggest that people's memories may be encoded in past language and that remembering happens in former ways of talking/thinking. In trying to return to a place that is gone forever, people may speak in the language spoken in that time/space. This is particularly the case when present-day correlates do not exist for terms such as "the ice man." The temporal heteroglossia that we identify in such cases is not carried out as much due to strategy as to necessity: what is intentional, poetic, and political here may be the very act of continuing to talk about a time and place that no longer exist.

In describing everyday life in Syrian Town, however, speakers use words that can be dangerous, for they sometimes do not have the same meaning in contemporary parlance. We noticed this early on in our study when we were taken aback by some of the language our speakers used. While speakers intend to convey the past as a better time, some of their *words* seem to undermine the picture they're trying to paint, so sometimes they hedge or backtrack to translate their words into the positive terms acceptable in the contemporary chronotope. For instance, while a student was interviewing Pam, she launched into a story meant to illustrate how there was no fear of others in the neighborhood. Her family's house had been down by the Lehigh River, and they would often entertain homeless people who would pass by.

> We were down by the one river, Lehigh River. Anyhow, that's where we were. Our backyards—we went down, when we got out of our yard and went down the road in back of our house, there was an ice house, that had made ice, there was garages for rent, and the water wasn't too far, the river was right there. So, and we had, they used to call them the *"bums."* . . . The people that drink a lot, and they don't work anymore, but they're always drinking. *"Bums,"* they're always— that's what we—that's what everybody used to call them. But I didn't like that name. And, there was one of them that was such a wonderful person. He was a professor before he got onto booze.

After using the term "bums," Pam exhibited discomfort in realizing that the term she had employed no longer has the same meaning as it did in her memory of neighborhood life in the past, and she struggled to explain the former significance of the term. She resorted to describing accompanying ideas and attributes rather than redefining the past word in contrast to its current usage. In this example, it seemed to us that Pam did not select a "past term" strategically to make a point; instead, it sounded unintentional, as evidenced by the way she paused to backtrack and explain what she meant. Thus, we argue that the past term emerged in relation to the topic Pam was talking about, without planning. The chronotope itself elicited a certain way of speaking.

This perspective also helps explain some of Joëlle Bahloul's findings. As she collected narratives about a specific Jewish Muslim household in colonial Algeria, she noted that her interviewees would use linguistic practices that they had previously used in the colonial era. Algerian Jews had spoken Arabic as their everyday language since medieval times; in 1870 they received French citizenship and gradually adopted the French language. French became the language for public interaction, whereas Arabic remained a language of intimacy and home life. In Bahloul's conversations with the Algerian Jews in the 1970s, their recollections included Arabic phrases, although the population now spoke French quite consistently: "The occasional use of the Arabic lexicon in narratives delivered in French is a form of re-enactment of past experiences: just as reconstructing the past requires rebuilding the past house, so it requires a return to past linguistic practice."[27] Again, returning mentally to a former chronotope entailed a reversion to the language of that chronotope.

We have already seen when Jerry backtracked to translate "white slavery" into contemporary language for Anna and when Martha asked about "the cat's meow." The speakers' repairs and metanarratives were partly due to the young age of several interviewers; the former residents of Syrian Town were not confused, unsure of their memories, or intentionally making statements to stigmatize a particular racial, ethnic, or socioeconomic group, as some of the words they used (such as "Syrian" and "bum") would suggest in typical usage today. On the contrary, they communicated the image of a diverse and very close-knit community.

It would have been misleading on our part to take the past terms at face value without recognizing their significance in the Syrian Town chronotope. On first glance, speakers using these words/patterns in talk could appear racist or simply elderly and nostalgic. The old terms could thus be taken to undermine what speakers want to communicate: how Syrian Town was "ahead of its time" and how the demolitions did not bring progress but the deterioration of the city.

It also would have been dangerous to assume that the speakers were intentionally selecting these particular terms to serve an argument about the past. As we have shown, in many cases speakers were not deliberately choosing certain terms for their rhetorical effect; instead, their words sometimes threatened the very claims they were advancing. In order to take seriously how these people relate to their past, it was vital that we endeavor to understand the past in its own terms. It was remembering the Syrian Town chronotope itself that caused speakers to resort to these terms; many of these terms were necessary to refer to places and concepts that, because of their demolition, had not acquired updated labels. The past terms emanated from the Syrian Town chronotope itself; our findings demonstrate how chronotopes can be generative.

History and Narration

For our interlocutors, language works as both tool and mnemonic that can involuntarily bring the past into the present moment. Our exploration of the ways elderly men and women narrate a former time and place they once shared demonstrates that linguistic artifacts, like the material objects our participants also treasure, serve as "signs of history."[28] Like a president's pen that brings citizens back to a landmark event, past terms evidence a lost world and help bring it back to life.

The most concrete manifestations of this past world are the place and shop names themselves, and much time was spent at each reunion swapping stories and reciting those cherished places. Former toponyms, while meaningless to later generations, are verbal artifacts. Raymond Williams explains that "the process of articulation is necessarily also a material process, and that the sign itself becomes part of a (socially created) physical and material world."[29] In narrating these place-names, interlocutors were connecting with each other, bringing new arrivals to the reunions into the remembering process. In turn, participation allowed individuals to identify themselves as bona fide members, for only former residents remember these places. Remembering together in this way yielded additional stories, which could proceed once the memory scaffolding, the reconstruction of the physical place, was under way. Past terms, including ethnic labels (Syrian), occupations (ice man), descriptive language, and former expressions (such as slouch hat, white slavery, or eyes as big as Orphan Annie's), are significant not only for their descriptive functions. These and other past terms help articulate the neighborhood—a specific place in a specific time—in the imagination of the speaker. In this way, temporal heteroglossia facilitates travel to a former chronotope, and traveling there may be impossible without temporal heteroglossia.

When speakers use older ethnic labels or such terms as "bums" in their spoken narratives about the past, the words are pulled out of their historical context, and the historicity and specific context of their speech is not easily traceable. At first, upon talking with these men and women about the old neighborhood, we were stumped: Why would people constantly describe a world as close-knit across ethnic lines while constantly labeling the ethnicities of the subjects of their stories in a fashion that by today's criteria would seem judgmental or even racist? It took us some time to recognize that in discussing a specific time and place, they began using the language of that time and place. Unable to resort to footnotes or special punctuation, however, our speakers had to find a way to accommodate the pastness of this language in their discourse. As we saw with Dorothy, she couldn't use "Lebanese" to tell her story about the nun, but in saying "Syrian," she was in effect citing herself and others in the past. Lacking an easy means of signaling that they are quoting themselves in the past, then, our speakers use the terms that ring true to the chronotope they are narrating, to that story world. The listeners, in turn, are meant to interpret these terms within that context as well. In contrast to the conventions developed by historians to key pastness—such as footnotes, special punctuation, and visible citations—*spoken* renditions of history must find other ways to clue listeners in. Using past terms is one mechanism for keying the past in speech; but when terms from the past emerge in conversation, an uninitiated listener is quite liable to misunderstand.

In this sense, spoken renditions of history (as opposed to written renditions) carry a particular kind of risk. The Syrian Town chronotope exerted a kind of agency, exerting itself on its speakers, as we have shown, and helping to generate the past terms people use to tell their stories. These past terms in turn carry their own power to help conjure up the physical space and time, the former context, in which they were used. But the very terms used to tell these stories can interfere with the telling, acting on both the speakers and their listeners in the present-day chronotope. Those who share the referent can capture the meaning, but those who don't may be lost or at least misunderstand, hence the regular repairs and metanarratives we encountered. The terms of the past became obstacles at times, detritus from a different era, potentially littering a narrative with confusion. In the end, we were only able to understand the underlying intent of these stories by paying close attention to the past terms themselves and, ultimately, translating them into contemporary ways of speaking.

As Hannele Dufva writes, the Bakhtinian notion of heteroglossia forces us to "re-interpret much of what is done with contemporary psycholinguistics," shifting toward a more dynamic model of remembering. Mental knowledge, she says, should "bear traces of [this] heteroglossia": "It may be assumed that *what* is known (certain words, forms, phrases) has to go hand in hand with *when, where* and with *whom* it is used."[30] In our data, the very process of remembering the old neighborhood, sometimes in a context that includes other former residents, seems to bring up the words from a different time-space, from a distinct chronotope, along with the mental image of the place; former linguistic patterns arise as people remember. The chronotope itself is generative, as we have argued. Memories of places and symbols of memories (in the case at hand, specific terms) are not decoupled from one another but perform the work of memory together; they are mutually constitutive and exist in relation to one another through process.

5. The Material of Memory

Stella is a dynamo. A petite octogenarian with short cropped white hair and large blue glasses, she has lived in a tiny ranch house in a nearby suburb of Easton for nearly forty years. We met her at her home for our interviews. After admiring her festive front yard, covered with real and plastic flowers and colorful gnome figurines, we were directed to her basement, where she had set out a lavish breakfast of pastries and coffee to enjoy as we asked her about life in the neighborhood.

A younger woman who had married into Stella's family encouraged Stella to share her family photos with us. Stella brought over a large green box from the bookshelf and opened it up. We first viewed large, cardboard-backed family portraits that were over fifty years old and discussed the people depicted: Stella's father in front of his Easton fruit store, right after he was released from the service in World War II, black-and-white portraits of dour-looking families in front of a house in Lebanon. Underneath dozens of more contemporary wedding photos was something altogether different: a stack of faded newspaper clippings, carefully cut, some pasted onto cardboard. We found image after image of the lost buildings we had been hearing about all these years taken at the moment of their demolition and reproduced in the local paper, gathered and stored with care along with images of her deceased relatives in a treasured cardboard box.

Stella's collection is not unique, and throughout this project we have been struck by the power of photographs of former streets and copies of the old telephone book pages for our speakers and the role of these items in generating recollections. We have also found that even the act of returning to the site of a speaker's childhood playground, now a parking lot but surrounded by its original fence, seems to elicit fleeting mem-

—Easton Press

View From The Harlan House

e southern section of downtown Easton basks in a summer sun. Shown   the intersection will be cleared as part of the Riverside Drive Redevel
"-the foreground is the intersection of South Fourth and Lehigh   opment Project area.
s, with the Moose home to the left. The residential area beyond

FIG. 10. South 4th and Lehigh before redevelopment. Image courtesy of Stella's collection.

FIG. 11. Demolition picture. Image courtesy of Stella's collection.

FIG. 12. Viewing remnants of the past. Image courtesy of Andrea Smith.

ories. These items activated for our interviewees the memories that they held, archived in their minds. Indeed, objects and places can trigger remembering, as Maurice Halbwachs noted long ago.[1] Objects and images of former places are physical points of connection in the present for our speakers, who otherwise only have their memories of these former places in common. But objects and places are more than material props for remembering when we view social life, subjectivity, and the material frame as all constituting each other. This chapter explores the ways place is both constructed by and integral to people's recollections of the past. Inspired by work on memory, place, and materiality,[2] we explore the role of objects and places in moments of collective and individual remembering and the way specific place-based details circulate.

Objects and Places as Signs of History

In *The Collective Memory*, first published in 1950, Halbwachs asked why people become attached to objects and responded that it is because "our physical surroundings bear our and others' imprint. Our home—

furniture and its arrangement, room décor—recalls family and friends whom we see frequently within this framework." Not only do objects circulate within a group of people, but also "each object appropriately placed in the whole recalls a way of life common to many men . . . [and] stand[s] around us a mute and motionless society."[3]

Objects often entered into conversations or were physically brought to reunions, where they served as clues to the lost Syrian Town world. Although many would be perceived as insignificant to outsiders, to the residents who brought them in, they "recalled a whole way of life." Across the years of conducting this research, actual items from the era of the neighborhood began to enter into our study as participants brought them in for us to see. These items were revealed with hushed tones as if we were being shown something sacred: one elderly woman carefully unwrapped a perfume bottle she had saved from an elite department store that was based in town and made sure that we took photographs. During another event, a simple paper napkin held special status. On it was printed an image of a now-defunct restaurant that had served neighborhood residents, and we were even given one of these last surviving napkins to keep; it was nearly tossed by a student helping clean out files who did not recognize its import. And then there were Stella's newspaper clippings: while for some they were just worthless scraps of paper, for her they were cherished portraits, the last remnants of a vanished world.

Like Jerry's description of the colored sidewalk or the hardy mint plant we discussed previously, these artifacts are "signs of history," vestiges from a former era.[4] They are items from the spatiotemporal context of the events to which they refer. As Richard Parmentier emphasizes, the value of such signs lies with their purported contiguity with the original temporal context; in Lisa Rasmussen's terms, their value lies with their "metonymic" properties, their "interconnectedness of different periods of time."[5] This was certainly the case with each of the items mentioned here—old bottle, napkin, or newspaper clipping—which were otherwise without value to the uninformed. As signs of history, these physical remnants carry an aura, a value, that stems from their ties to and origins in a former place and time.[6]

As we have noted, the abundant past terms that we discussed in the previous chapter can be viewed as playing a similar role. As "artifacts"

FIG. 13. Signs of history: bottles from the past. Image courtesy of Andrea Smith.

The CIRCLON
EASTON, PA.

FIG. 14. Signs of history: napkin from the Circlon Restaurant. Image courtesy of Andrea Smith.

from a previous time and place, these terms emerge from a prior era, triggered by memories of that time and place, that chronotopic envelope. Not only do they index a former time, but in so doing, they also bring the past into the present.

Places, due to their materiality and the fact that buildings and other structures often not only last but outlast the humans who built them, also connect present and past and can be viewed similarly as "signs of history" that play an essential role in reconstructions of the past.[7] Halbwachs was especially sensitive to the role place plays in this regard. His insights are consonant with ours at first in that he emphasized the mutual constitution of places and peoples: "The group not only transforms the space into which it has been inserted, but also yields and adapts to its physical surroundings. It becomes enclosed within the framework it has built. The group's image of its external milieu and its stable relationships with this environment becomes paramount in the idea it forms of itself, permeating every element of its consciousness, moderating and governing its evolution." What happens, then, when this relationship between group and place is severed? In Halbwachs's view, it is this image the society forms of itself that matters: space becomes a predominantly symbolic resource: "The reason members of a group remain united, even after scattering and finding nothing in their new physical surrounding to recall the home they have left, is that they think of the old home and its layout."[8] While Halbwachs here recognizes, as we do, the role of place in reconstituting a community after its dispersal, his approach differs from ours in a fundamental way. In these passages, he moves from a dialectical perspective that explores the mutual constitution of people and place to a focus on "society"; ultimately, in his view, place serves primarily as a symbolic resource that allows "society" to develop an awareness of itself. In his view, the old home is a mnemonic, as it reflects the social relations that it contained; the physical urban framework gives a group an "image of itself." Mindful of Latour's warning against theories that rely too easily on a presupposed "society" and any construct modified by the word "social," we will explore this question—the power of place for people removed from it—further. What is it about objects, space, and remembering former places that motivates our speakers so?

Reconstructing the City

When people talked to us about now-gone shops and streets, they seemed to be attempting to reconstruct the whole neighborhood, right there before us, with stories rich in former place-names. Visual details accompany these stories. Whether it was Agatha recounting in lavish detail the house that "redevelopment" took from her and her husband, or Rosemary remembering walking down to the neighborhood each day after school, looking out over the steep steps down into Syrian Town ("You looked down and there it was, all spread out: to me, it was heaven"), people often seemed to be trying to paint a picture of that lost world for us. In many ways, this recounting of former shops and streets, even by repeating their names, helped create the scaffolding necessary for further recollection, the places to which they could attach their narratives.

Given the dwindling numbers of people who share the same geographic framework, it is no surprise that when former neighbors reunited, they especially enjoyed relating this information or even comparing notes. They often talked about former places in an excited, quick-paced dialogue, delighted, it seemed to us, to encounter someone with the same knowledge base, as illustrated in the previous chapter. Some of these conversations continued unabated for over an hour. Place-names were shared in fluid back-and-forth volleys as speakers together narrated the former shops and streets back into being. Note, for instance, the ways two brothers and their friend narrate the neighborhood:

HOWIE: Remember Easton had Stocker's Music Club?
ALBERT: Yup, yup. Ken Stocker's over there.
HOWIE: And right next door to that, I think it was a typewriter place that I think used to be, Pennsylvania Tailors. Somewhere over there. Uh, uh, on um, 3rd Street, used to be Deluxe Restaurant on the corner—
ALBERT: Deluxe, the Crystal Restaurant.
HOWIE: Crystal, okay. Then there was Rapp's, uh drugstore—
ALBERT: The pharmacy.
HOWIE: Then the Sweet Shop. And then there was um, a furniture store.

ALBERT: Okay, what side of the street?

HOWIE: This side [*makes gesture*], not the other side where Lipkin's and whatnot, but on this side. And then they um—

ALBERT: I remember Carelli's, the appliance store.

HOWIE: Okay, okay.

BILLY: Carelli's on the other side, though.

ALBERT: Okay, I didn't know which side Charlie was talking about.

BILLY: He was going all the way down.[9]

"Which side are you talking about?" "He was going all the way down." Statements such as these suggest that retracing buildings had occurred more than once to these men, either individually or together, and we witness here the men trying to reconstruct, building by building, the shops that were found on one side of a given block.

On another occasion, a gentleman shared a written list he had constructed from memory of all the stores in a several-block radius. He even recopied the list to sort the shops into categories, counting up for us the number of shoe stores, furniture stores, and so on that had been located on the now-razed streets.

An activity organized by the interviewees themselves confirms the significance of this knowledge base and these place-names to our interviewees. Members of the displaced community volunteered to help us plan reunions and became "the planning committee." As part of a Taylor School neighborhood reunion held in October 2011, MaryAnne, a seventy-eight-year-old African American woman, wanted to administer a "pop quiz" and invite people to answer questions about the old neighborhood. Of the twenty-four questions she generated, none of them had to do with the Taylor School itself. Rather, the majority of the questions were about details of the city's structures, asking for the names of streets and establishments.

As MaryAnne read the questions off, other reunion attendees were intent on answering them correctly. Some got frustrated, yelling "Ohhhhhh!" or saying "I give up!" because they couldn't remember the names. Some people disapproved of certain questions, claiming they were too open-ended, yelling out, "Too many answers! Too many answers!" before MaryAnne even finished saying the question. Later, as she revealed the answers, the room was silent and tense, people hardly breathing as they anticipated her response, and many former residents got angry when their answers were wrong. The room became a tizzy of frustration, with people yelling over one another. "She's right!" "No, before the curve was West Street, after the curve it's called Front Street!" "She didn't say Centennial!" "Why didn't she say Centennial?" "No, that was across the street!" This cacophony left MaryAnne feeling defensive and the reunion attendees feeling scattered and aggravated. We saw then our interviewees' serious interest in concretizing what was no longer: borrowing Joëlle Balhoul's phrase, "memories turned into fetishes."[10]

The need to recount the former layout of the town began to seem an essential part of these reunions. In many ways, in talking about Syrian Town, participants were engaged in "place-making," "retrospective world-building," which anthropologist Keith Basso has described as a "universal tool of the historical imagination." As he writes, place-making is a way of "constructing history itself, of inventing it, of fashioning novel versions of 'What happened here.'" While the place-names used in Syrian Town place making in no way matched the intricacy and poetics of those of Basso's Western Apache consultants, we found again and again our need to "start with the names," as Nick Thompson told Basso, "learn the names of all these places."[11]

Learning the Names: Ruptures in Visualizing the Past

Since so many of the stories our speakers shared were rooted in place, knowledge of the city's former geography was essential for successful communication, and unfamiliarity with this geography sometimes posed an impediment in conversations and interviews. In fact, during the early years of this research project, we sometimes felt we were engaged in a crash course in Easton's lost cityscapes. It is only now, after several years of research, that when we hear someone remember walking down the South 5th Street steps, we feel that we too can picture that part of town.

The inclusion of new researchers at the end of the project was helpful in confirming these insights, for one of the best ways to demonstrate the significance of place to remembering is to consider conversations in which the different parties do *not* share the same place-based knowledge. Recorded interviews conducted at the end of the study involving

FIG. 15. Mingling of the generations. Image courtesy of Luis Gomez.

students enrolled in Smith's course in ethnographic field methods and collaborative anthropology, A&S 244, who were brand-new to the topic and usually new to the area sometimes provided insightful moments of real disconnect, further illustrating the significance of place and especially place-names in these narratives.

In her very first interview, a student asked MaryAnne to describe where she grew up:

STUDENT: I guess we can start with, um, basically, I guess tell me about how you grew up and what community you were a part of in terms of your ethnicity, and how that played a role in how you grew up.

MARYANNE: Well, actually I didn't live too far from here. You don't know anything about Easton, do you?

STUDENT: No . . .

MARYANNE: Do you know where Larry Holmes Drive is? Everybody knows where that is!

STUDENT: Where what?

MARYANNE: Larry Holmes Drive.

STUDENT: [*laughs*].

MARYANNE: Do you know how to get to P-burg?

STUDENT: To where?

MARYANNE: Philipsburg.

STUDENT: Philipsburg? Yeah.

MARYANNE: Okay, so—I lived down in that area.

STUDENT: Okay.

MARYANNE: That was called Front Street. And everybody just helped out everybody [she begins to describe her immediate neighbors].

In this example, MaryAnne starts out with a contemporary street name, Larry Holmes Drive, which was created after urban renewal out of Front Street and which now runs around the city parallel to the river. When the student doesn't recognize that street name, MaryAnne tries to get her to imagine the bridge that crosses the Delaware River, leading into the town on the New Jersey side, Philipsburg, which is known to locals as simply P-burg (see map 1). The student doesn't recognize that name either, but when MaryAnne finally tells her it is Philipsburg, she is oriented. It is only then that MaryAnne commences to talk about her life growing up in the neighborhood.

In another conversation, a different student talks with Howie and brothers Albert and Billy, and their conversation focused on sports. One of the men mentions having gone back into the gym at the Wolf Junior High, which has been closed for decades, and finding it exactly the same as when they played there as kids.

STUDENT: That's cool that it's exactly the same for you guys, the way you remember. Was it just the basketball court?

ALBERT: Where?

STUDENT: The Wolf School.

ALBERT: It's mainly basketball, yeah. You know the building we're talking about?

STUDENT: I don't think so.

BILLY: Down here, on 2nd Street! When you leave, just cruise by.

ALBERT: Take a left and go down that street. The first big building you see to your right. It has this big arch way up on top and steps going up there that always looked the same.

STUDENT: So did they build that after redevelopment?

BILLY: No, no.

ALBERT: That's been there long before. Amazingly enough, it wasn't torn down.

BILLY: But if I remember correctly, I think maybe our parents might have gone there. The Wolf is <u>that</u> old.

Albert then jokes to his brother, to much laughter around the table, indicating the "pastness" of these places: "She's probably thinking, 'Oh you some old farts! I need to go to another table. Talking about dinosaurs pretty soon!'"

This section again indicates the desire on the part of the participants to connect the interviewer into visualizing their world. While the student doesn't seem hampered by her lack of knowledge about the Wolf School today, from this conversation, it appears that the men are, and they proceed to give her detailed directions so that she can walk down and see the school for herself right after the interview. As with Mary-Anne's conversation, the men couldn't seem to let it go and couldn't carry on with their storytelling until their interlocutor had some sense of the physical location they were discussing.

In the next example, we see a few instances in which the interviewee queries student participants about their knowledge of local geography. In the first excerpt, the student interviewer's knowledge is passable, and the speaker proceeds. In the second excerpt, she is lost, and the disconnect makes the interview challenging for both parties.

Martha often rooted her stories quite explicitly in location. Sensitive to her listener's reaction, she often stopped to make sure interviewers were following her and asked whether or not they were familiar with the location under discussion, as is evident in the following two excerpts:

MARTHA: Let me tell you about the library. Like I said, we didn't have much growing up, so we'd go to the library, which is where it is. Know where the public library is? Familiar with the public library?

STUDENT: Mmm.

MARTHA: OK, well the children's entrance was up on 5th Street, and I could not understand how they would let us out of that library without paying for these books . . .

In the next excerpt, Martha tries to relate a significant moment in her life, a time when she was far from town when suddenly a World War II era blackout occurred, forcing her to walk home several miles in the dark:

MARTHA: Oh, I can remember one time during a blackout. During the Second World War. There would be a siren, and you had to turn all your lights out and put the shades down. But, uh, I remember somehow or another someone took us to Bushkill Park. Now, Bushkill Park is a good distance from downtown Easton. Do you know the Bushkill Park?

STUDENT: Near the Bushkill Falls?

MARTHA: No, that's near the Poconos! [The Poconos are a mountain range about an hour north of the city.] Bushkill *Park*, over near Tatamy Road [she pauses as she tries to find some commonly shared reference point]. Oh, a few miles from downtown Easton. Near Palmer Township [she seems to give up and just continues with her story]. And we had to walk home in the darkness. Can you imagine doing that today?[12]

In this example, the location, Bushkill Park, is important for her story, for to travel from there back to town, she had to walk for miles along a spooky wooded road that runs along a creek. The location is clearly lost on the student, and Martha works hard to find some common point of reference, finally concluding, "Oh, a few miles from downtown Easton." Throughout this ninety-minute interview, there are hesitations and even frustrations when Martha can't relate her story fully to the students because they don't have a connection to the places she is referencing, the places essential to communicating her stories.

Finally, we offer an example of the opposite situation: the excitement an interviewee experiences when his interviewer unexpectedly shares a common point of reference. Bill, of mixed German descent, participated in several reunions and enjoyed engaging with students. He attended Taylor School with many of the other study participants; however, his childhood home was outside the demolition area and thus is still standing. Moreover, it is located quite close to the college the student researchers attend. We have audiorecorded several conversations with Bill and can discern his telling interlocutors the address of his childhood home on more than one occasion, only to find that his interlocutors have no idea where it is. In the following instance, however, his interviewer shared this knowledge, and the excitement is palpable even in the recording transcript:

> BILL: I lived at 3XX Spring Garden; that's really 4th and Spring Garden. If you've ever seen Leo's barbershop at the corner there . . .
>
> STUDENT: I actually just went there a couple of weeks ago.
>
> BILL: Did you?!
>
> STUDENT: Yeah.
>
> BILL: He's a good, he's a great guy.
>
> STUDENT: Exactly.
>
> BILL: Well, we rented that storeroom!
>
> STUDENT: Okay.
>
> BILL: That's, that's our house, was our house, and Leo paid, paid rent to us. I don't know who he pays the rent to now, but that was it. So I made that walk from 3XX Spring Garden over here to Ferry and Lehigh every day. In fact, I did it twice a day, because we went home for lunch.[13]

This excerpt illustrates the significance to Bill that his interlocutor shared some modicum of local geographic knowledge, and this shared knowledge seemed to give Bill permission to outline his daily childhood journey to school in some detail.

Getting It Right

We have seen how knowledge of the geography of the former neighborhood engages its former residents, leading to quizzes and casual verbal challenges that punctuate reunions and even the reunion-planning meetings. Gaps in this knowledge can thus challenge and frustrate. From these vignettes, we gain a real sense of how difficult it must be for neighborhood survivors to talk about their childhoods at all with so few people left who share the same mental map of the lost cityscape, especially now that all the reference points have been removed. In such a circumstance, the names themselves take on a vital role: people not only wanted to situate their stories within the city's former geography but also wanted us to get the place-names right.

We also encountered this desire for precision regarding the typed transcripts themselves. Throughout this study, we have sent transcripts of the recordings back to participants for their review and correction, and this practice continued with the student class. What we find remarkable is the degree to which corrections on the returned transcripts single out not punctuation, general spelling, or content, but place-names. These corrected transcripts indicate both student unfamiliarity with this lost landscape and participant desire for precision. "Pumford Club" is circled or crossed off, and in the margins is written "Pomfret Club," "Karusso's" is carefully changed to become "Caruso's," "North Hampton Street" is corrected (it is Northampton Street). "Greasers? Store" becomes "Reeser's," "Ekluand Terrace" becomes "Heckman Terrace," "Lobb" becomes "Lave," and so on.

We are reminded of Keith Basso's discussion of the importance of pronouncing place-names correctly when he was admonished by an Apache consultant, "Tell him he's repeating the speech of our ancestors!"[14] At reunion events, it was the name itself that seemed powerful. In reciting the names of the physical structures, speakers seemed to be bringing back to mind the whole lost world, building by building. Place-names, as vital past terms, come out of the past, reflecting it, but they also serve to re-create it, bringing it to life in the present. Here, particular words help constitute a collective framework for remembering in the absence of the built environment.

Embodied Memories

We would now like to move beyond an understanding of places and objects as props for remembering, as resources providing the group with an idea "of itself," as Halbwachs suggested.[15] Instead, we embrace a dialectical approach to materiality that considers the ways people, objects, and places can be viewed as mutually constituted. All of the senses are involved in emplacement, as Steven Feld has noted: "As place is sensed, senses are placed; as places make sense, senses make place."[16]

We feel that the focus of these elderly men and women on the materiality of life in yesteryear is significant and that the speakers engaged in MaryAnne's competition are doing something more than testing each other's knowledge or claiming to be "authentic" Syrian Towners. They are reemplacing themselves, rebuilding through past terms the material framework needed to complete their own biographies. We return for a moment to Allan Pred, who argued that the structuring of space is inseparable from the structuring of society: the production of history, the becoming of places (and objects), and the formation of biographies are "unwrapped in one another."[17] And as Alfred Gell writes: "Material objects are not just signs or a medium for making relations among people possible but are integral to how people develop a sense of themselves as subjects and of the reality of such abstractions as society."[18] We must move beyond what some term "cognitive memories" to what Paul Connerton calls "habit-memory," "a knowledge and a remembering in the hands and in the body; in the cultivation of habit it is our body which 'understands.'"[19] In what follows, we argue that the "emplacement" of people in their neighborhoods stays with them—in them—long after the neighborhood is gone.[20]

In her study of the use of everyday objects in remembering school days, Rasmussen suggests that remembering can be viewed as surpassing solely mental processes, and she is interested in "nonverbalized" memories as well. In her examples, the people she interviewed sometimes found it easier to imitate their school-day behaviors than describe them in words, as when they weighed "an invisible pen between their fingers." She suggests that because various objects were woven into a time-specific context of everyday school life, they served as "contact zones," allowing people to reexperience or re-create life in the present: "The sensual aspects of the memories analyzed seem intrinsically linked to the very materiality of the objects."[21] We see this with a whole host of embodied memories that were bantered about in a freewheeling fashion during reunions and interviews. In people's stories, objects and places sometimes converge, for they often described detailed physical features of the urban landscape: the steepness of local streets, the cold of the snowy sidewalks. As archaeologist Julia Hendon explains, physical settings remind people of the way it *felt* to be part of that setting. She describes how seeing the Acropolis at her field site reminds her both of the physical sensations of climbing it and of the inter-subjective relations experienced there.[22]

Subjectivity and materiality come together in striking ways in the stories we heard about childhood activities such as playing sports or going to school that involved *paths* and *projects*, concepts we borrow from Allan Pred. Paths are actions or events making up the existence of an individual, conceptualized as an unbroken continuous path through time-space. Projects involve the "coupling together in time and space of uninterrupted paths of two or more people" toward some wider goal; examples here include "hanging out at the train station" and "going to school." We note that many such stories involve not only specific places and material objects but also the body: people reminisce about sliding down steep steps in the winter months on cardboard or even just their pants on the way to school, with hilarious miming of coming to school with wet bottoms as a result. They talk about various city obstacles, remembering a gate with slats wide enough for them to slip through but that grownups could not that the children used to "escape" from menacing policemen. Many of the stories we heard reveal an embodied memory of the city streets.

Stories we heard about school involved all the senses. When one student asked Edna and Mark what they remembered about the Taylor School, Edna immediately replied, "All them steps in the school—don't you remember all them steps that you had to go up to go upstairs to the principal's office?"

The playground was also a big topic of conversation, and speakers shared stories that recounted the physical experience of playing at that spot. In one conversation, Edna asked Mark, "You know what I remember best about Taylor School, which was right here? Didn't it seem like we had a big yard, like the grassy part?" Mark asks if she's talking about the playground, and she confirms this is the case: "Yeah, remember when they showed movies there? We used to sit on the ground, and they used to show movies there." Mark concurs, "Yeah, right where this parking lot is now. *This* was a playground, and there was another one on the other side. One was for the girls and one was for the boys at recess." Several minutes into the conversation, Mark returns to describe the playground in more detail: "Like I said, we played here [*points in a direction*] with the boys' and girls' playgrounds, and the playground at the time had grass. And we used to play marbles there [*points*]. And we played marbles and basketball there, right against the fence. It was small, but it was a place to play."

Perhaps the most consistent of such school tales involve memories of the corporal punishment experienced at school: whether the smart of the ruler brandished by teachers or the "whack" students heard when the principal punished a boy for throwing snowballs. (HOWIE: "Remember Mr. B. and the big paddle he had?" ALBERT: "Oh, man! It must have been made of hickory or something, because you used to *hear* that in classes.") Former pupils of the Taylor School also talked about clapping the erasers for teachers after school and the pride a student experienced when asked to be monitor; donning the white sash at the end of the school day signified this responsibility and honor. They seemed to sit up straighter when recounting these tales. Stories of lunchtime, another mutually constituted project, included a discussion of the luxurious taste of cold chocolate milk that was experienced only when the wealthier students didn't show up that day. ("Well, let me tell you, I'd get that chocolate milk, I'd siphon it up, take a little bit, let it go back down [the straw], just so it would last long [*laughs*]. Isn't it funny how you remember certain things like that?")

Sports too can be seen as Predian projects and sports teams as their constitutive communities of practice. One afternoon, Howie, Billy, and Albert reminisced at length about playing on a team started by a friend's older brother, a high school teacher with organizational talent. He created the "EUCC" for the boys of the neighborhood. The men were unclear about the underlying team name that led to that acronym. ("Howie, what does that stand for?" "It was a derogatory statement—it was Easton

United Colored Coon, or Easton United Civilized Cult. I'm serious!" he responded.) They proceeded to talk at length about their mismatched outfits when they played on a local basketball team: "It was ragtag, a ragtag team. Everybody had different-colored socks, different-colored shoes, whereas the other people, okay? We played outsiders, they had everything that matched. And I'd like to say we were an ass-kicking team [*laughs*], but, uh, that'd be false. Anyway, I'm just thinking back now just talking about it, shoot." We heard people remember how they stuffed their shoes with cardboard in the winter to protect their feet against the icy cold and played with footballs made out of newspaper bunched together and tied up with string. "Stories about being poor, they were," as Mark told us. Being poor as the body remembered it.

Children playing the same sports and games like jump rope, quoits, and marbles are similar to Hendon's statements about the experience of participating in common crafts: "Each of these crafts represents a form of knowledge that is transmitted across generations within communities of practice and among adults and children brought together through marriage, coresidence, proximity, trade, feasting, work exchanges, and other formal and informal mechanisms. This is an embodied and often tacit knowledge that is enacted through the mastery of the tangible and the abstract. It is learned through experience, repetition and engagement of the senses."[23] In Pred's terms, these projects brought together people, places, and objects with *paths* that intersected even for a brief moment. And, perhaps most significantly, even if they did not traverse these paths simultaneously, the people we met had traveled across the same spatial coordinates at a particular moment in time. As former residents of the same neighborhood, they were all engaged in a relationship with the same physical space, an underlying relationship that unites them today.

Locus of Concern: Reconstructing the Neighborhood

Of all places significant to remembering, the home is perhaps the most emotionally magnetic, generating dreams and affect that persist for a lifetime.[24] Symbol of "our very humanity," the home is a vital mnemonic.[25] It is a site of socialization, of cultural knowledge and unstated learning.[26] As Hendon writes, "Domestic places are meaningful backgrounds because they are physical and social spaces that actively contribute to the development of identity and memory from which local and localized histories grow."[27]

Many anthropologists focusing on memory explore this power of the home and the ways it is involved in shaping certain kinds of people. Daniel Miller cautions against focusing solely on the house as symbol or locus of social relations, however, and suggests that we not ignore its very materiality.[28] Interestingly, materiality is almost entirely the focus of our speakers' discussion of their former homes, as we have elaborated in chapter 2. We have already suggested that one explanation for such a focus could be in reaction to the fact that the quality of the structures was impugned directly or indirectly by the pro-redevelopment city leaders; our speakers thus continued to defend the physical structures as a way to call into question the entire renewal project. This certainly seemed to be the case in Agatha's detailed descriptions: "It had a picture window, wood-paneled doors—they were expensive—I had a dining room, a special dining room, I had a kitchen up to date and everything." Dorothy became animated when she described the demolition process in detail. She talked about the old fireplace mantelpiece: "Old wood, I can't remember the name of the wood, but old wood. They went in there, and they took a two-by-four, and they broke the mantle!" Recall this man's vivid description of his childhood home: "Where the windows were, they had marble. We had solid oak steps going up, three stories plus a full basement. They were built with double brick—they were fantastic buildings, large buildings, large rooms." His discourse might also contain an implicit commentary on the present day, for at the time, we were meeting at the tiny single-story ranch house where he had lived on the fringes of a rural township since being forced out of the Syrian Town neighborhood.

At the same time, we rarely heard about the domestic life these homes contained and fostered; instead, most such stories took place in the wider neighborhood. This may reflect the fact that people spent much more of their childhoods out of the house than is common today. An emphasis on the neighborhood rather than the household could also be interpreted as a reflection of the public nature of the speech events we have been recording. However, when we return to our emphasis on a *processual* understanding of place and its emphasis on individual paths and communal projects, more of the profound meaning of the neighborhood emphasis becomes clear.

In Hendon's exploration of the meaning of domestic spaces in Honduras, she considers the interpersonal relations those spaces fostered. She writes that people living in large multifamily compounds "were enmeshed in repeated acts of commensality, ritual, and cooperation that would have created a sense of common or shared identity. At the same time they were constantly reminded of the ways in which they differed from one another in status, wealth, role, gender, age and so on." This is partly because remembering is an embodied process, and these repeated activities helped "create communities of practice among coresidents and between groups living in different residences."[29] In our stories, households sometimes appear, and certainly some people talked about parents, siblings, and other relatives. But it is significant to us that the elderly speakers were so outward in focus. At least in the reunions and other large gatherings, it is not the family, the household, or the ethnic or religious group of which they were a part that serves as the unifying force but something larger, a place constructed only in their stories. It is the neighborhood itself—the streets, the buildings, the school, the overlapping and intersecting childhood and young-adulthood projects and their communities of practice—that matters.

This brings us back to the nature of the population we are considering in this book and their un-group-like nature. Even though the people reuniting claim clear and distinct "nationalities," a membership in ethnoreligious and racial subgroups, as we saw in chapter 3, it is interesting that they are reaching across these subgroups to engage together as individuals. We are reminded of Fred Myers's description of Pintupi (Australian Aborigine) place-making practices. He discerns that the concept of "one countryman," all the people with whom an individual regularly camped, is a coresidential group whose composition varies with each individual. As Myers explains, "The concept is egocentric, with each person's set being unique to him, including many who did not always live with the same residential group." It is *coresidence* at a common site that matters and even fosters a sense of ownership of that place for Pintupi: "Regular residence in an area also gives one a claim to identification with—and potentially an 'ownership' of—the 'country' (*ngurra*), the named places where one lives."[30] Similarly, in our example, it is shared participation in overlapping communities of practice and residence at specific sites—the school, playground, streets, train station—that connect this disparate group of individuals, even for fleeting moments at the reunions.

It is worth reiterating the role of language here. In Pred's study of Swedish villages before their dramatic reordering in the eighteenth century, he analyzes the way each village could be viewed as "worlds apart in a common world" due to its relative isolation. As a result, despite the common basic linguistic structures, there were dramatic "place-to-place divergences in language," and he compares the lexicons of three villages as illustration. The reason for these local divergences in language is clear: language, materiality, and embodied memories are intricately intertwined, as words and practices are "unbreakably cemented together." As Pred writes, "Personality and consciousness do not exist independently but are the complex by-product of past path-project intersections." He goes on to outline the relationships that people are engaged in not only with places but also with other living things and objects through the participation in projects: "When participating in those activities at precise local sites and more or less fixed temporal locations, and thus having his or her participation in other activities and projects constrained, the individual daily undergoes experiences, interacts with other people, acquires or reinforces competencies and encounters symbolically laden, inanimate objects, ideas and information otherwise would not have come his or her way in exactly the same form." In this regard, a sense of place is conceived of "not as something that stands on its own but as a phenomenon that is part of the *becoming of individual consciousness* and thereby inseparable from *biography formation* and the becoming of place."[31]

These insights help elucidate the energy and connections that seemed instantaneous when attendees met, sometimes after decades, and the fact that these connections seemed just as real among people who had not known each other specifically in the past. In Pred's terms, they participated in common projects (school, sports teams, hanging out at the train station) at precise local sites (the Taylor School, the boys' playground, the train station lobby) but sometimes on different days or during different years. They journeyed along paths that intersected with the same physical terrain (walking to school down the huge 5th Street steps) but at different moments in time. Being rooted in the same place, they spoke the same idiom and connected with each other along terms from the same chronotope that reflected the unique local cultural geography and social categories. The reunion participants attended the same school, but sometimes different years, and they traveled the same streets and attended the same movie theaters—not necessarily with each other but with a fellow reunion participant's older brother or younger cousin. We might see the neighborhood itself, then, as a network of intersecting individual paths gathered over a given period of time that link together distinct but interrelated biographies. It is not only that these interlocking communities of practice took place in this space but also that they helped constitute it, all the while helping to develop the childhoods and adulthoods—the biographies—of the speakers we encountered. Thus, it was not the "society" that held them together, that holds them together today, but their common *individual* relationships to a common neighborhood, a common space, their use of a specific local language that pins them back down to the same space and time, that returns them to the same chronotopic envelope.

The implications of this insight are wide-reaching: since it is place—that is, traveling along a common path in the same geographical coordinates—that creates the community, it is the place itself that gathers, that assembles.[32] It is through their common understanding of their shared relationships to a common place that something we might call "society" is formed. Places do not reflect an already-made society back to itself, as Halbwachs might have argued; instead, place itself (not to be confused with space) makes "society."

It follows that the severing of people and place will be highly disruptive. For individual residents, the missing place—the neighborhood in our study—becomes a kind of phantom limb. The desire of our participants for meetings and reunions, which provide a space for them to look at old photographs, to find clues that confirm their memories, and to speak the former places back into being, reflects this truncated relationship. The reunions thus can be interpreted as efforts at healing a wounded subjectivity, an attempt to revive a sense of place that is such a foundational element of individual consciousness and biography.

As a result of the mutually constitutive experience of place, with people and objects developing together, people are engaged in relationships not only with each other but also with place, with former ways of living and of speaking. Their subjectivities and their very language biographies were constituted through their interactions with and within specific buildings, and they remember where a curb changes color, a dusty playground, and a patch of mint plants. By traveling down the street in their mind's eye or through collective discussions with people who knew these places, they are weaving back together interlocking sets of communities of practice and rebuilding the relationships that made these practices possible in the process. It is not in rebuilding a former set of social relationships that their connection to the old places becomes evident; in fact, it is their severed relationship to place that instigates this rebuilding of social ties. In the final chapter, we will consider how this whole process, this reassembling, may be not only rejuvenating but also, fundamentally, political.

6. Nostalgia as Engine of Change

> There is a dream that somewhere out there—in the space of
> marginalia and eccentricity—there are "places" still caught in
> the ongoing density of sociality and desire. Places to which
> "we" might return—in mind, if not in body—in search of
> redemption and renewal.
>
> KATHLEEN STEWART, *A Space on the Side of the Road*

"We never used to lock our doors." "We were all family." "You were everyone's child." "We didn't know color." The depictions we heard of neighborhood life in yesteryear were so consistently positive that they raise the question of nostalgia, a widespread trope that resonates in so many other contexts.[1] We might challenge many of the tales' golden tint and consider age, asking if these assertions reflect a more widespread experience of the very old wishing to return to their childhoods. Or we might ask if this nostalgia reflects a more generalized condition in contemporary times: perhaps it is the neoliberal present itself that calls up memories of Syrian Town, reminiscent of the town Egeria that Kathleen Stewart writes about, "an old timey place indexing a nostalgia for a time and place apart from the cities and the postindustrial present."[2]

In this chapter, we explore nostalgic evocations of Syrian Town. We argue that rather than simply representing a reflection of a people unhappy with their present circumstances,[3] nostalgia can carry motivational force, spurring residents to find ideals in the past that they wish to continue into the present. In neighborhood reunions, we see challenges to the existing order, nostalgia not only as "redemption and renewal," as Stewart has written, but also as a call for change, nostalgia as "back-talk." Serving as conclusion, this chapter comes full circle as we see the role the neighborhood reunions play in helping to rebuild the world that former residents thought they had lost forever.

Nostalgia for the Past in the Present

Often portrayed as a reaction against rapid change associated with the forces of modernity, a reflection of the "disorganizing and all pervasive economy of late capitalism," nostalgia is seemingly everywhere.[4] A neologism created in 1688 by Swiss medical student Johannes Hofer to depict a physical ailment experienced by Swiss mercenaries experiencing "home-loss," nostalgia is often depicted as "perverse," "pathological," or a reaction to overly rapid change.[5] Yet anthropologists emphasize the need to ground particular nostalgic evocations in specific circumstances. As Kathleen Stewart writes, "It depends on where you stand." "Nostalgia," she adds, "is a cultural practice, not a given content; its forms, meanings, and effects shift with the context." While for some it is part of a "schizophrenic exhilaration" related to the bewildering and exhilarating hyperreality of the contemporary moment, from the perspective of people living on the "margins," "nostalgia is a painful homesickness that generates desire."[6]

Because commentary on the past often contains an implicit or veiled critique of the present moment, we can better understand the meanings being relayed about Syrian Town and the wider messages these stories provide when viewed within the contemporary context. The experiences of our speakers since leaving Syrian Town have real bearing on the implicit meanings of their stories. So much has changed in Easton since the 1960s, yet our speakers kept returning to a few key points of contrast with the town of today. These include the emptiness of downtown, the racial homogeneity of the contemporary order, and the fact that *then* and *now* seem to be populated by different types of people.

"It Was a Lose-Lose"

The devastation of Syrian Town was part of a wider series of projects that altered Easton in dramatic fashion. By 1966, 146 buildings had been destroyed on 13.5 acres in the Lehigh-Washington Street project, displacing 83 families and 14 businesses.[7] Most of the land was ultimately sold to the Easton Housing Authority and not to the builders of high-rise luxury apartments, as planners had promised. Construction of two senior

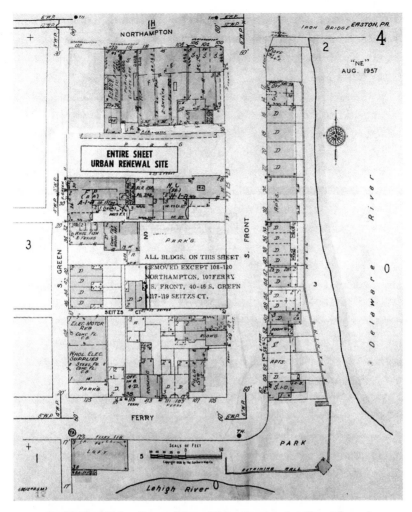

MAP 4. *Entire Sheet Urban Renewal Area.* "Once you start leveling, where do you draw the line?" Demolitions occurred so frequently and covered so much of the city's downtown that it became difficult to adjust the city's Sanborn maps accordingly. City administrators instead began editing the maps with blanket statements, as we see here. All of the buildings in this sheet aside from those indicated were removed as part of the Riverside Drive renewal project. Insurance Maps of Easton PA, Sanborn Map Company, New York, 1958, Sheet 4. Reprinted/used with permission from the Sanborn Library, LLC, and the city of Easton PA, Bureau of Planning.

citizens' homes, a nursing home, offices for the Easton Chamber of Commerce, and privately owned subsidized senior citizen apartments followed. The spectacular wealth and spaces promised by city planners never transpired.

Although this project attacked the center of the Lebanese neighborhood, it did not destroy it completely. Blocks of Syrian Town remained, particularly on the other side of Lehigh, South 5th, and South 4th Streets. These blocks were soon eradicated with the city's next large project, the Riverside Drive project. Undertaken between mid-1966 and 1971, this project involved the destruction of 173 buildings on 22 acres, including the spiritual centerpiece of the Lebanese community, its church.[8] In the process, 79 businesses and 128 families were uprooted, some of whom had been dislocated just a few years earlier by the Lehigh-Washington Street project. By 1977 the Easton Redevelopment Authority had paid over $11.6 million for the acquisition of property in its five urban renewal projects, leveling over 870 homes in the process and leaving the city's appearance "irreversibly changed."[9] Only a few months later, city planners seem to have had second thoughts, for their annual report of that year commenced with a poem lamenting the ease and destructiveness of "bulldozer" renewal.[10] Yet the damage was already done.

Many of the former residents admitted to us that they may be better off financially as a whole, especially those people who settled into new homes in the surrounding suburbs. But all suggested that the city as a whole suffered. One man laughed at how officials promised the city great financial benefits: "They got rid of hundreds of homes, and built what? A Quality Inn? I know you need to make reservations years in advance to stay there!" he sarcastically joked. Another man, when asked who benefited from redevelopment, practically shouted at us:

> How could you say anybody benefited when the government made little money for their homes, and the people who took that money and purchased other homes had a tough time in coming up with new mortgages?! They were working hard all their lives to support their families: who would benefit? The government lost and the people lost. And in the long run, what happened in Easton? Heavy crime, no income coming in, no revenues, who benefited? It was a lose-lose,

you know. The only guy who I could see benefiting was the guy who ripped them down and made money! That's all.

Once a crowded, mixed-use neighborhood, noisy with factories, peddlers hawking their wares, and its multitude of residents, the site is now largely empty, a blank abstract space cleared to create new places for capitalist exploitation but on which little was built. Most of the few private enterprises established on former Syrian Town lands, a Perkins Restaurant and a movie theater, have since been razed, and an even larger parking garage is in the works. But it is not just the buildings that people miss. As Gastón Gordillo so trenchantly observes, "Destruction disintegrates not just matter but the conditions of sociality that define a particular spatial node."[11]

"I Walk Down the Street and I Don't Know Anyone"

The sociability of the former order was greatly missed. In our speakers' stories, this sociability is linked to the pre-Walmart economic order, which involved a densely packed, multiuse downtown with residents walking to and from work at nearby steel and textile mills and other local industry that was buttressed by a myriad of independent shops.[12] Note, for instance, how Mark discusses mom-and-pop stores: "They had a lot of businesses. Thomas, they had a little store. There were four to five people who were Lebanese who had stores. The stores were *nice*. Everybody *knew* everybody. Not like it is now. I walk down the street and I don't know *anyone*." In Mark's view, the "niceness" of the stores is directly linked to the rich social life they brought to the city, not to the products they sold (in fact, on this occasion, as in many of such discussions, we do not know *what* the stores sold, just the owners' names and sometimes their ethnicities). And it is this sociability that seems to be most lacking in the contemporary order ("I don't know *anyone*").

The experiences people had since the 1960s of living in more ethnically homogeneous or ethnically unmarked neighborhoods has real bearing on their stories as well. Rather than fostering economic growth downtown, the renewal projects that attacked Syrian Town helped accelerate the processes of suburbanization already under way, fostering a major reordering of the social landscape as Syrian Town's neighbors were sorted or sorted themselves largely along racial lines. According to our informants, some Lebanese and Italian families found new homes uptown, but most moved to rapidly growing suburbs in surrounding townships, and we were able to corroborate these impressions with data from later city directories (1965 and 1970). Due to the housing discrimination of that era, inscribed in federal legislation and banking practices, most people of darker skin tones moved (often several times) to crowded sites in the city center or to the south side of town, on the other side of the Lehigh River, as members of the NAACP had predicted and as city reports amply document.[13] As a result, a black/white binary solidified in Easton, accelerated by the renewal projects, as occurred in so many other cities nationwide.[14]

Our speakers' emphasis on the *ethnic diversity* of Syrian Town and on themselves as "ethnic people" stands in marked contrast to the cityscape today. While they talked to us about life a half-century ago, our speakers are of course living in the twenty-first century and thus are aware of contemporary understandings of race and the national models of personhood that circulate through the media and shape so much of public understanding. It is *especially* in the context of the contemporary social order that ethnonym-inflected narratives of everyday life in Syrian Town are "reportable" or "tellable": they are describing something worth telling.[15] In discussing this former place and time in this way, our speakers again and again are making evaluative statements about the present setting, creatively constructing the contemporary world as homogeneous and other. Certainly our interviewees contrasted the ethnic diversity they had experienced with the lack of diversity in their communities today. We can see this in Gloria's discussion when she said, "It was a really nice place to grow up, nice area to grow up. 'Cause you got the mixture. Maybe if today people could understand one another's . . . ethnic people, maybe it'd be a nicer life, a nicer world." She seems to be associating the positive qualities of the neighborhood with the ethnic mixture itself and suggests that the world could be a nicer place if the understanding she gained from such an upbringing was more widespread in the present.

Interviewees also recognized that the people who populated their recollections challenged today's stereotypes associated with the same social categories. Some nonblack speakers felt the need to qualify their stories even while telling them. Sometimes when they talked to us about "blacks," they seemed to feel the need to contend with the specter of a contemporary black stereotype in order to communicate effectively about the past, and they interrupted their own stories to comment on the gap between the meaning of that social category in the past and today. For instance, Agatha stopped herself to explain that the black subjects of her story were "not like the Afro-Americans that you see now and stuff like that. They were like high class." She also commented on the superior quality of the homes owned by her black neighbors on several occasions. When we interviewed Mark and Jerry, black men in their eighties, they too contrasted today's violence with the harmony of the past. After hearing the former mayor describe Syrian Town as ridden with social ills, we asked Mark if he thought that the neighborhood had been associated with criminality. His response was quick: "No way, *no way*," adding with laughter, "Maybe a few kids who were mischievous stole some cupcakes or something." During a different conversation, a woman named Jennifer explained, "People say that the blacks today can't get along with anyone, but things were different then." By describing the peaceful relationship between Syrian Town residents, including black residents, the interviewees reinforced the image of the tight-knit community they had lived in. Any tensions surrounding the label "black" did not seem to come from within the neighborhood but rather from changing political implications of the term since the neighborhood's demolition.

A Different Kind of Person

There was an overt moral quality to the stories we heard about Syrian Town; it was a place inhabited by a certain type of person: hardworking, working class, generous in spirit. When Rosemary, a woman in her sixties, relayed walking down to the neighborhood after school and described it as "heaven," we asked what was so nice about it. "The very simple thing of sitting out on the street," she replied. People would sit on the streets together, children would play together, talk together, and it was this sociality she loved to remember. People described a "safe" place peopled by hard workers. Shopkeepers worked long hours; one woman told us that she felt safe day or night because there was always someone awake, working: walking home from her late-night job at a local bar, she would see the lights coming on at the bakeries. This was also a working-class part of town where people made do with little, where a hot dog was "the cat's meow." As we have argued, the widespread use of ethnonyms serves to index membership in this humble, working-class stratum: if you lived in Syrian Town, you were an "ethnic" and came from one of the local "nationalities," in marked contrast to the homogeneous, white, and wealthy College Hill residents.

As they narrate Syrian Town, our speakers are positioning themselves as people who cared for one another across racial and ethnic divides. With the demolitions, the Easton landscape became segregated: effectively this was the conclusion of one chronotope and the beginning of another. Before redevelopment, drawn plans of the futuristic Easton pictured an ultramodernist, airy space with vast expanses and clean lines. What the drawings did not capture was the radical racial segregation that the changes put into play. Besides the fact that the physical improvements to Easton were never realized, the area's social deterioration is a powerful counternarrative to the promised urban "renewal." As Agatha related to us, "In those days, the Lebanese, the Jews, the Italians, the Afro-Americans . . . all lived mixed, one right after the other. Now, we went to each other's funerals, we went to each other's weddings, we were there for each other, and that is something that I will never forget." This sense of community is often explicitly contrasted with the latent violence and isolation of the contemporary city.

Creating a Nonplace

Another feature of the site of the old neighborhood, as is not uncommon in "modern" urban areas today, is its apparent *lack* of history. In the name of progress, in the attempt to create modernity, new material forms camouflage the relationships, motivations, and ideologies that have built them. While city planners envisioned grandeur, we find here a perversion of the capitalist logic so richly represented by others.[16] Rather than the "destructive production" that Gordillo writes is inherent in the capitalist cycle, a process that creates "vast amounts of wealth, objects and places" through "ruination," the spatial destruction carried out during midcentury urban renewal projects was the end point; often, the promised "production" stage never came to pass.[17] Wrought through the use of eminent domain, a speeding up in the purchasing of homes, and their rapid and complete clearance, the production of destruction never yielded the promised spectacular spaces after all. Rather than "destructive production," then, destruction was perfected; because rebuilding was an elusive and poorly thought out part of the equation, it never fully transpired in Easton, and instead these spaces are largely bare, peppered with low-budget public projects, now old and in dire need of structural attention.

Henri Lefebvre writes about the evolution and hegemony of "abstract space," which includes the "world of commodities, its 'logic' and its world-wide strategies." Within this space, he writes, "the town . . . has disintegrated."[18] Meanwhile, as Stewart's ethnography poetically describes, history still seems to live on in the devastated, marginalized sites, while "central" places grow "vague and interchangeable," what James Kunstler has termed "the geography of nowhere." Stewart writes, "It may seem strange that it is in these most marginalized, out-of-the-way places that place seems to matter most while the places lodged firmly in the center of things grow vague and interchangeable. Strange that these places so devastated by history retain the marks and memories of the past while in the suburbs the sheer timelessness of the straight line of progress spreads like oak wilt from house to house."[19] Interestingly, Syrian Town had once been "in the center of things" but was made completely "out of the way" through its removal. And yet, like other such places, for some, it still "matters most."

Nowhere is space so devoid of the marks of time than in the suburbs, where many of our speakers now live. These "master planned communities" graced by "picture-perfect simulacra of homeyness emptied of history and memory" hover at the margins of many of our stories.[20] One story told so many times it must contain some truth is that the move to the suburbs killed off the older generation prematurely. We heard especially from Lebanese interviewees that the move devastated a whole generation. The oldest who were "removed" were the most likely to be the Arabic-speaking immigrant generation, who walked across the neighborhood to their church on a regular if not daily basis. Once in the suburbs, they found themselves isolated in an alien land, miles from their church, their friends, their children, waiting for relatives to drive them in. They became depressed. We heard from a city official whose first city job was working for the Redevelopment Authority checking in on those who were relocated. He told us he never got over seeing people sitting in their brand-new kitchens sobbing in utter despair.

While at Sami's bar, seventy-five-year-old Josie said that of course, people who had to move "probably got better homes, better property, but it wasn't the same." She told us a story about one of her black neighbors who managed to purchase in the suburbs. He showed up at her home out of the blue one night around 7:30 and seemed upset. She asked what was wrong. "I'm going cotton picking crazy! Josie, I'm going cotton picking crazy," she remembered. She asked him why, and he said, "Where we moved, there's no one to talk to, no one is out on their front porch!"

Urban Renewal as Place-Loss

Concern for lost places continues to mount as our ability to reshape both urban and rural landscapes seemingly overnight advances with each passing year. In the United States, there are few spaces "safe" from rapid and potentially total transformation, as long-term residents of Easton learned when they faced the loss of land through eminent domain in the 1960s. Today's threats comes from similar federal renewal policies, as well as proposed gas pipelines bringing Marcellus shale gas to ports along the eastern coast of the Atlantic Ocean. Lands may be lost again through eminent domain, and expulsions continue to threaten, again motivated by promised riches. Sometimes it seems that only a few places—perhaps national parks, military installations, and toxic waste sites—are islands in the storm threatened with complete overhaul. As James Bielo writes, "The threat of placeless-ness is an American social fact."[21]

Personal and cultural losses experienced by people removed from places have been the focus of a rich and ever-evolving scholarly literature and have continuously motivated artists and writers. Many anthropologists document the creative ways people have endeavored to cope with such dislocation.[22] Whether refugees from Hurricane Katrina and other natural disasters, or dislocated due to wars or racial and religious discrimination, people removed from their homes spend their lives finding ways to cope. A friend and Katrina exile told Joshunda Sanders one day in tears, "No one can ever know what it's like to have their home taken from them and wake up one day knowing it doesn't exist anymore." Sanders writes, "I wanted to tell her that some of us *do* know, and that it is a miracle we survive at all." Herself homeless and displaced more often than not, Sanders remembers fondly a project she lived in in the Bronx, "poor nation of old buildings and gutted dreams." Nevertheless, she has always seen that building as home, and since leaving it, "everywhere I've lived, I have taped a New York City subway map and a Bronx bus map to the wall about the space where I write. I am so nostalgic and fond of the Bronx for the gritty gifts it gave to me."[23] Sanders's preservation of the layout of her former gritty home is reminiscent of the actions taken by the people removed from Syrian Town, who carefully store old napkins and display archaic photos; in light of the personal losses that result from urban renewal, we have found it useful throughout this book to view urban renewal as a form of place-loss.

Alterations to cityscapes dislocate, as Maurice Halbwachs knew well. We find it significant that his first in-depth research was a study of the aftermath of the dramatic nineteenth-century reshaping of Paris, which led to the displacement of over three hundred thousand residents. This first research experience may have had some bearing on his ability to empathize with those whose lives are shattered by urban change. He wrote in a later work, "Inhabitants pay disproportionate attention to what I have called the material aspect of the city. The great majority may well be more sensitive to a certain street being torn up, or a certain building or home being razed, than to the gravest national, political, or religious events." From the perspective of the individual, the effects can be devastating: "Any inhabitant for whom these old walls, rundown homes, and obscure passageways create a little universe, who has many remembrances fastened to these images now obliterated forever, feels a whole part of himself dying with these things and regrets they could not last at least for his lifetime."[24] Statements such as these suggest that he gained a real understanding of individual subjective response to urban dislocation through his interactions with the displaced.

Some of our speakers described the advocates of Easton's redevelopment as "fanatics," as "radicals," motivated by some kind of utopian vision of a better world. However we might characterize their vision, it was not exclusive to this small city: in cities across the United States, very similar plans were carried out in very similar neighborhoods. The destruction of La Calle, so eloquently documented in Lydia Otero's study, targeted a Mexican American neighborhood at the heart of Tucson, Arizona, during almost the same years and using nearly identical methods: outside advisory bodies that helped develop the plan, argumentation buttressed by earlier housing codes, and the development of public relations informational brochures with images depicting "good" and "bad" housing to help convince the electorate. And like the Lehigh-Washington Street project, Tucson's Old Pueblo District targeted the most densely populated, predominantly ethnic neighborhoods in the city. A consulting firm from Cincinnati had written a blueprint in the 1940s in which "blight" meant both unsanitary conditions and "the intermixing of racial and ethnic groups." However, as in Easton, Otero found that city officials and newspaper editors ultimately "avoided discussing race"; instead, the pursuit of urban renewal targeting largely a community of people of color did so "indirectly, through inference and innuendo."[25] And like Easton's "Lebanese" neighborhood, this was really a highly mixed neighborhood, with Chinese and African American residents who found it one of the few places they could live.

In fact, nearly any narrative about race in the contemporary United States will have strands tied tightly to the country's midcentury urban renewal frenzy. Black and Latino ghettos, white suburbs: these distinct social experiences are not two different stories but parts of the same story, interconnected elements of a wider whole. While the story told about the nation's largest cities is quite well known, with massive devastation as highways bisected the known world, what is often missed in this wider narrative sweep are the everyday experiences of people who were forging a multiethnic and multiracial world together before the great divide. We rarely hear what life was like in richly integrated cityscapes before the great segregating aftermath of so many such projects. What were the meanings of ethnicity and race to individuals living and working together in neighborhoods united instead by their class standing? As we have documented here, people living in a small Lebanese/Italian/black neighborhood in the heart of a burgeoning city had ways of talking and thinking about difference that differed from the wider norms. These meanings likely differed in other urban areas as well, possibly according to the particular ethnic composition represented in any given neighborhood and the wider state or regional racial and ethnic politics within which that neighborhood was situated; as John Hartigan reminds us, difference is a "local matter."[26] Language-centered research on other ethnic enclaves is likely to yield fascinating results, furthering our understanding of the diversity and longevity of local ethnonyms, race, and difference. Master narratives about the evolution of whiteness will surely become more nuanced as a result.

A vital question for today is how the meanings of race in such communities, united by class but multiply ethnic, were shifted, distorted even, when the class connections were lost. Relocation to the suburbs, which allowed so many of the Italian and Lebanese families in our study to move solidly into the middle class, was not an option available to most of the black families we interviewed. This has had lasting consequences: as senior citizens, some of our interviewees live in homes they have now paid off in the older suburbs surrounding the city and will likely live out their lives there. Others, and in our study this means mostly the black residents, have moved, often, from one public housing project to the other, sometimes more than once over the course of a given year of our study. These people likely would no longer see themselves as members of the same class stratum, even if they had been so during their time in Syrian Town. How we might further understand the consequences of this unlinking of class, ethnicity, and place for shifting notions of race is a topic of vital concern in this racially divisive country today.

We have emphasized in this book the need to consider the legacy of expulsion in the United States. It can be easy to fall into a presentist trap, leading to a sense that it is only now that matters, only now when the masterminds of neoliberalism have ramped up their destructive forces. We hope that we have shown that projects that took place over fifty years ago also matter today. This insight gives us pause; to hold in one's mind the disruption caused by a small project in this small city and then multiply it by the number of people across this country influenced by similar kinds of urban renewal projects is simply staggering.

Affixing a Price

What does it mean to remove people from their homes? Why should we consider how this removal took place, and why does it matter? City officials and business owners in some cities across the country may revel in the recent economic growth spurred on by urban renewal projects quite similar in timing and rationale to that which swept away Syrian Town. If these projects represented progress, should they be lamented? The renewal proponents we spoke with indicated, rather harshly at times it seemed, that the city had compensated people for their losses and had done so generously. One woman insisted that they were all better off now, even if people wouldn't admit it. Her statement echoes that of some of the interviewees in James Robert Saunders and Renae Nadine Shackelford's oral history of Vinegar Hill, a black neighborhood lost to renewal in Charlottesville, Virginia. As one of their informants, William Jackson, told them, "In point of living arrangements, I think it was an improvement. People got more modern housing with running water inside and that sort of thing." Yet others were not convinced. Another informant, Teresa Price, explained: "During eminent domain, they compensate people in terms of the value of the real estate in city hall. And when you get that compensation, we don't get enough to reinvest in what you would call a better kind of real estate. So, they didn't feel like they were ever adequately compensated."[27] Is the value of a home or a neighborhood so easily measured? In their essay about urban renewal from the 1960s, Wilton Sogg and Warren Wertheimer suggest, "In the relocation of individuals and families displaced from a renewal area, it is crucial that the ultimate objectives of urban renewal be considered. These persons must be relocated in such a way as to prevent the areas to which they move from becoming new slums," adding that the "future development of the city" is also a concern. As Saunders and Shackelford write, these statements expose a potential conflict: "What is beneficial for the city and what is beneficial to people subject to relocation might very well be two different things."[28] In other words, defining what is "beneficial" and what counts as "progress" for the collective frequently privileges some of its members at the expense of others; in considering such efforts, it is worth articulating what the stakes are and for whom.

In fact, people subject to eviction through eminent domain often report that any amount of financial compensation could not be enough. In the case of Tucson's La Calle (mentioned above), Otero reports there were multiple lawsuits as residents tried to block relocation; when that didn't work, some people were physically forced out of their homes after they refused to leave. As Saunders and Shackelford write regarding the relocation of blacks from Vinegar Hill, "If nothing else, one thing is certain. Neither black property owners nor renters were ever adequately compensated for the loss of their cultural center, a place that had somehow found a way to flourish in the midst of a citywide community that was repressive by its very nature."[29]

The means by which people were forced to leave matters as well. The use by their own government of eminent domain to seize their homes still riles former Syrian Town residents today, leaving lasting consequences regarding how people view specific city officials, as we have seen. Some claim they have boycotted city businesses since then, thus taking partial responsibility for helping to accelerate the city's economic downfall. Likewise, many residents of La Calle were angry and resentful. One woman talked about watching "it all go down": "It was bad. . . . People weren't very happy. They'd been there all their lives. It was quite a trauma for us, for everybody."[30] Otero, as well as Saunders and Shackelford, relate stories about elderly people who could not bear being relocated and who died prematurely, as our speakers too have described. As one woman said, "If the city wants to kill old people, they should shoot them and not take their houses, families, and friends away from them."[31] Others felt "betrayed" or "harbored feelings of fear, loss, disappointment and resentment." Some of Saunders and Shackelford's interviewees reported a similar sense of disillusionment and indicated a distancing from local government and the political process more generally. The Reverend Elisha Hall, a city council member long after urban renewal decisions were made, found that the consequences of eminent domain and the removal of people from their homes reverberated, shaping people's attitudes toward future projects long after the fact: "It's certainly affected the people's attitudes toward anything that the city will try to do. Each meeting we get into about some plans what we're going to do, they say, 'Uh-uh, it's gonna be just like Vinegar Hill. You took our houses from us, especially the older people, and we ended up over in the projects.' And that's where some of them are and some of them will die."[32]

FIG. 16. Pedagogical discourse in action. Courtesy of Andrea Smith.

Nostalgia as "Back Talk"

In her powerful study of the making of southern whiteness in the segregated South, Grace Hale considers the lasting consequences of such a social order: "It is necessary to highlight the collective cost, the damage segregation has done to the collective ability to conjure our broadest cross-racial connectedness, and to acknowledge the resulting poverty of the attempts to imagine an inclusive America."[33] Our speakers, having grown up in a rare racially integrated neighborhood, seem well aware of these costs. It is for this reason that Syrian Town nostalgia is a kind of "back talk," what Stewart describes as a response to "America's mythic claims to realism, progress, and order."[34] Our speakers challenge first the city leaders who had thought redevelopment would make some kind of sense, and second the direction the society has been headed in as a result of so many such projects. We often wondered if there was something political in the content of the stories we were hearing. Over time, it became clear to us that it was the fact that people *met up* and *discussed* this past place, continually bringing it back to life, that was the primary political act.

These reunions have not faltered but keep building, and the involvement of undergraduates in these reunions is both a response to and an accelerant of this building momentum. After Anna left for graduate school, Andrea kept receiving additional emails and images from community members "to share with Anna." When she decided to continue the project by bringing whole groups of undergraduates to the meetings, this inclusion of a new, much younger audience may have granted a further sense of purpose to the recollecting of past times, and the meetings sometimes seemed reminiscent of "pedagogical discourse," a form of historical discourse Charles Briggs observed in exchanges between elders and their juniors in rural Hispanic communities in New Mexico. Briggs notes a dialectical structure to this kind of discourse, moving back and forth from back then and today, between *antes* and *ahora*, punctuated by "periodic synthesis, which consists of the derivation of a basic moral value that underlies the opposition." As Briggs explains, "The elders' point is not simply that this value was present antes and is absent ahora, but that such values are of equal importance to survival nowadays." The elders are exhorting the younger listeners "to internalize these values and to reflect them in their behavior."[35] Similarly, by meeting with us on so many occasions, by gathering together the various disparate residents, the former residents of Syrian Town offer instruction, whether through their stories about the value of walking in times before the automobile or the importance to a community of regular work, or indirectly, by simply gathering together their racially and ethnically diverse group of friends and former neighbors. By gathering, "reassembling," they are piecing back together their beloved community, one that city officials had once deemed "blighted." And as we have related, these reunions are not isolated events, for even prior to our involvement in organizing them, other reunions had been under way for years, including more generic high school reunions but also weekly meetings at a Lebanese-owned bar.

By defining themselves in ethnic terms, by returning to the ethnicity-infused patterns of identification, former residents of Syrian Town are also directly challenging contemporary ways of speaking. By claiming *nationality* as a significant ground of difference, they are rejecting the racialized language of the contemporary order. By reuniting, the participants are gathering together in one space members of the disparate ethnicities, re-creating what people at the time had even suggested was a bit too much integration. By talking with each other and the younger generation, they are "talking back" to the city elites who destroyed their neighborhood. In recollecting a lost world, they are finding ways to rebuild it.

Rebuilding Worlds

We have documented in this book the psychic losses experienced as the result of dislocation and theorized why removal from place can linger in the individual consciousness. We want to call attention to the implication of these findings for understandings of memory as process. First we must acknowledge that remembering can be viewed as an "authenticating act,"[36] and our very presence may have assisted in this authentication. There can be no ethnographic study of remembering that is not altering the way something is recorded, narrated, and thus remembered. Nonetheless, to talk about the past together was cathartic for our speakers. Narrating and remembering are in a dialectical relationship: as Elinor Ochs and Lisa Capps emphasize, while memory influences how we conarrate experiences, narrative practices influence how experiences are encoded or revised in memory.[37] Our work extends their insight to demonstrate that language itself cannot be understood as prior to memory, nor can memory be understood as prior to language, for the specific language used—words, phrases, and speech practices (like the pervasive use of ethnonyms and place-names)—plays a vital role in the act of remembering. So too do material objects, as we have shown.

We want to also consider implications for an anthropology of history.[38] Our findings suggest that individual memories are narrated and understandable in relation to space, objects, and the embodied memories they are integral to, as well as the linguistic matrix within which individual memories are embedded. Having grown up in the same physical location, rooted largely in a similar class background, and sharing a common social location within the wider community, former residents are able to reconnect despite not having shared identical experiences, identical individual memories. Their relationship to one another in the present is defined by a common setting for a previous portion of their everyday lives, now shared only through remembering.

Our findings strongly commend a view of both people and place as coconstructed; we are reminded of Pierre Bourdieu's notion of *habitus* and an embodied way of being in the world that does not easily leave an individual.[39] Former residents of Syrian Town keep returning to the lost place, imagining it so vividly that it seemed to us like a collective phantom limb that they returned to, again and again, as we have described. Their way of being in the world was shattered through the demolition process. Their Syrian Town *habitus* remains in the language patterns we have documented that persist despite their life's peregrinations. Writing about the "unconscious" quality of *habitus*, Bourdieu quotes Émile Durkheim: "In each of us . . . there is part of yesterday's man. . . . Yet we do not sense this man of the past, because he is inveterate in us; he makes up the unconscious part of ourselves. Consequently we are led to take no account of him."[40] Applying this statement to language use, we can see the "yesterday's man" within our speakers as his language brushed up against that of today's man, leading to disjunctures and repairs. And for former residents, reconnecting to the "yesterday's man" in one another after decades seemed easy, due precisely to this shared *habitus*.

The reunion attendees felt a deep connection with one another, even though many of them had not known each other while living in Syrian Town. Since many people were meeting for the first time at the reunions, the commensality they felt in these contexts is not based on former ties *to one another personally*. Rather, what they share is a similar distant connection to the old neighborhood and, with that, particular language practices. What binds these people together is not having shared an identical experience or identical episodic memories (such as participating in the same strike) but their shared embodied memory of place, the interlocking communities of practices, a memory of once living in the same rich, multiethnic social world, and their shared social location within a wider cityscape.[41] Much of this is traceable in the language that they use, as we have seen.

Language plays a central part in reawakening "yesterday's man." By talking about the former social matrix (past terms for ethnic groups, use of reported speech), the former class location (in using old ethnic labels to distinguish themselves against the local elite), and physical matrix (place-names), former residents are uniting along shared points of connection and in many ways re-creating a past world as they rejoin now fifty years after dispersal. While talking about this past time and place, they enter a story world that generates other old-fashioned phrasings. At the same time, in speaking this former world into being, they narrate chronotopes that in turn act as "instigators," generative of former ways of speaking.

In talking about Syrian Town, no single individual, volume of text, or particular location is the site where all memories of Syrian Town reside. In her ethnography of Latina youth gangs, Norma Mendoza-Denton finds that pieces of material culture and linguistic practices help instantiate a type of "distributed cognition" that binds gang members together in the absence of an official archive.[42] Past terms elicited through temporal heteroglossia played a similar role here. One former resident reported, "Some people cried when it [Taylor School] was torn down because it held their memories." But since Syrian Town was demolished, people's memories of it have not ceased: they continue to bear the imprint of where their memories "took place."

When we look at the role played by the "past talk" of our interlocutors, in speech the past is continuously entering into the present quite literally. We find it less useful to try to determine which takes precedence, language or memory, for as we see in these instances, their deep interrelatedness is evident. As we have shown, past terms sometimes even surprised their very speakers, who have to work to use them effectively to communicate in the present day.

No past terms were so significant to our speakers as those necessary to describe the former neighborhood's very physicality. The toponymic past terms bound the speakers together to the former place-in-time in two distinct ways. By denoting a piece of the neighborhood, these place-names are in a synechdochal relationship to the wider area, with the part standing for the whole. At the same time, as terms ripped out of the past, they are in a metonymic relationship with the former time, touching it, as it were, serving like Lisa Rasmussen's "knots" to link past and present.[43] Place-names connect speakers back into the Syrian Town chronotope along axes of both time and space.

The rememberers of Syrian Town speak to the close intersection of history, materiality, and personhood. Cultural practices don't leave a person but remain as a kind of historical reservoir that persists into the present. Not only do individuals contain past selves, but the historical is traceable and even formative: in this case, it is this historical matrix that unites people in the present. The effervescence of the reunions suggests that often trivialized, marginalized language practices, along with the memory of the context in which past terms were used, are enough to unify. This community of rememberers, many of whom are now pursuing new interpersonal relationships with one another, are in fact *only* connected to one another in the present. Two individuals, both from Syrian Town, know each other today—even if they never met before. Membership in a shared past chronotope is enough for these people to make their history together, to coconstruct it, to actively rebuild a shattered world in the present through recollection.

Notes

1. Ethnography of the Expelled

1. Gans, *Urban Villagers*; Gelfand, *Nation of Cities*; Hartigan, *Racial Situations*; Hirsch, *Making the Second Ghetto*; Judd, *Politics of Urban Planning*; Massey and Denton, *American Apartheid*; Sugrue, *Origins*.

2. On the role language plays in signaling the past, see Dick, "Imagined Lives"; Eisenlohr, "Temporalities of Community"; Eisenlohr, *Little India*; Inoue, "Temporality and Historicity." For work on materiality and memory, see Hendon, *Houses in a Landscape*; Miller, *Materiality*; Miller, *Material Cultures*; Rasmussen, "Touching Materiality." For a processual understanding of place, see Pred, *Place, Practice and Structure*.

3. On historical consciousness and an anthropology of history, see Stewart, *Dreaming and Historical Consciousness*, 1–9. For historical consciousness as a form of "distributed cognition," see Hutchins, *Cognition in the Wild*; see also Mendoza-Denton, *Homegirls*, 178. And for linguistic terms and material objects that serve as "signs of history," see Parmentier, *Sacred Remains*.

4. Aside from students named in full, names of individuals are pseudonyms.

5. See Smith, "Place Replaced"; Smith, *Colonial Memory*.

6. Smith, "Place Replaced"; Smith, "Settler Sites."

7. Smith, "Mormon Forestdale."

8. Smith and Scarpato, "The Language of 'Blight.'"

9. Sassen, *Expulsions*, 1, 2, 76.

10. For a discussion of supermodernity, see Augé, *Non-places*.

11. Von Hoffman "Study in Contradictions," 318; Gelfand, *Nation of Cities*, 208.

12. Gelfand, *Nation of Cities*, 212, 156.

13. Zimmer, *Rebuilding Cities*, 13.

14. Gans, *Urban Villagers*; Gelfand, *Nation of Cities*; Judd, *Politics of Urban Planning*; Kaplan, *Urban Renewal*; Petshek, *Challenge of Urban Reform*; Teaford, *Rough Road*.

15. Schuyler, *City Transformed*, 7.

16. Fourcade, *Habiter l'Arménie*.

17. Although we consider language and materiality together in this work, one limitation of our study is that we do not address the materiality of language to analyze characteristics of linguistic form such as code choice, vowel quality, pitch variation, or turn shape. These material elements of linguistic practice have proven revealing markers of style and stance, and they enable analysts to get beyond a bias toward the referentiality, which only accounts for a fraction of the semiotic work involved in communication (Silverstein, "Shifters, Linguistic Categories"; Silverstein, "The Limits of Awareness"). Explicit attention to these features would be a fruitful direction for future study by linguistic anthropologists, whose methods elicit the data necessary for that type of analysis. Such an approach promises to contribute crucial additional layers to the perspective on oral history and social memory that we seek to advance here and could prove particularly key in developing a nuanced theory of the temporal shifting that defines narration about the past and its social effects.

18. Hartigan, *Racial Situations,* 14.

19. Ethnic and racial labels and choosing whether or not to capitalize terms such as "black" and "white" are topics of real import and current intellectual debate. In *Everyday Language of White Racism*, Jane Hill elects to capitalize both terms to make a point about the socially constructed nature of race. In our work, we usually employ "black" to designate African Americans in this community, as this is the autonym employed by our interviewees who self-identified in this way. Because our interlocutors downplayed race as a factor in their neighborhood and social relations, we retain the lowercase usage throughout this text and treat the word "white" the same way. Neighborhood data are compiled from *Polk's Easton (Northampton County, Pa.) City Directory . . . 1963* (Boston MA, 1963), from which we developed a house-by-house database of neighborhood residents prior to demolition. Once the businesses (14) and vacant apartments (14) were eliminated, 141 residences remained. Former residents themselves attributed ethnicities in focus-group settings; these ethnic labels were in turn checked against the individual census records.

20. Bayor, "Another Look"; Brodkin, *How Jews Became White*; Guglielmo, *White on Arrival*; Hirsch, *Second Ghetto*; Hirsch, "E. Pluribus Duo?"; Jacobson, *Whiteness of a Different Color*; Ignatiev, *How the Irish Became White*; Kazal, *Becoming Old Stock*; Roediger, *Wages of Whiteness*; Roediger, *Working toward Whiteness*.

21. Jacobson, *Whiteness of a Different Color*, 8; Guglielmo, *White on Arrival*; Hirsch, *Second Ghetto*.

22. Bayor, "Another Look," 13; Myrdal, *American Dilemma*; see also Guglielmo, *White on Arrival*, 59.

23. Hartigan, *Racial Situations*, 14.

24. They were identified as "Turk," "Ottoman," "Syrian," "Armenian," "Assyrian," and "Arab."

25. Hooglund, "Introduction," 3.

26. Gualtieri, "Strange Fruit?"; Karpat, "Ottoman Emigration"; Hitti, *Syrians in America*. Considerable numbers of Muslims arrived even before 1900 and may have tried to pass as Christians (Karpat, "Ottoman Emigration," 183).

27. When the US Census Bureau first used a separate "Syrian" category in 1920, there were 51,900 people so identified (Karpat, "Ottoman Emigration," 181). See also Hooglund, "Introduction," 12; Naff, *Becoming American*.

28. For details of this 1915 court case, see Gualtieri, "Becoming 'White.'" For anti-Syrian discrimination, see Conklin and Faires, "'Colored' and Catholic"; Guglielmo, *White on Arrival*; Shadid, "Letter to the Editor," 47.

29. Only a few studies explore the effects of renewal on racially integrated neighborhoods. See McKee, "Liberal Ends"; Pritchett, "Race and Community."

30. Lefebvre, *Production of Space*; see also Gupta and Ferguson, "Beyond 'Culture'"; Harvey, *Condition of Postmodernity*; Harvey, *Justice, Nature*; Low, "Spatializing Culture"; Massey, *Space, Place, and Gender*; Rodman, "Empowering Place."

31. The term "multilocal" is from Rodman, "Empowering Place," 647.

32. Lefebvre, *Production of Space*, 10–11; Harvey, *Condition of Postmodernity*.

33. Lund and Benediktsson, "Introduction."

34. Raffaetà and Duff, "Putting Belonging into Place," 331; Renfrew, "Towards a Theory," 23; DeMarrais, "Materialization of Culture," 20.

35. Raffaetà and Duff, "Putting Belonging into Place," 331.

36. Myers, "Ways of Place-making," 99.

37. Myers, "Ways of Place-making," 105.

38. Pred, *Place, Practice and Structure*, 6, 2.

39. Pred, *Place, Practice and Structure*, 10, 21–22.

40. Pred, *Place, Practice and Structure,* 17, emphasis added.

41. Bakhtin, "Discourse in the Novel."

42. Hendon, *Houses in a Landscape*, 96, 125, 129.

43. Koptyoff, "Cultural Biography"; Renfrew, "Towards a Theory," 28.

44. Renfrew, "Towards a Theory," 28.

45. Koptyoff, "Cultural Biography"; see also Appadurai, *Social Life of Things*;

Hoskins, *Biographical Objects*. This literature is rich and ever-changing. Key sources include Gell, *Art and Agency*; Miller, *Material Cultures*; Miller, *Materiality*. For useful reviews, see Hoskins, "Agency, Biography and Objects"; and Meskell, "Introduction."

46. Halbwachs, *The Collective Memory*. Text quotes are from his *On Collective Memory*, 41, 38.

47. Irwin-Zarecka, *Frames of Remembrance*. See also Burke, "History as Social."

48. Anderson, *Imagined Communities*; Brow, "Notes on Community"; Hobsbawm and Ranger, *Invention of Tradition*.

49. Popular Memory Group, "Popular Memory," 207; Abercrombie, *Pathways of Memory*; Alonso, "The Effects of Truth"; Boyarin, *Polish Jews in Paris*; Holsey, *Routes of Remembrance*; Price, *First-Time*; Swedenburg, *Memories of Revolt*.

50. For tales from residents of Lebanese origin, see Smith and Scarpato, "Language of 'Blight.'"

51. Hutchins, *Cognition in the Wild*; Mendoza-Denton, *Homegirls*; Latour, *Reassembling the Social*.

52. Hutchins, *Cognition in the Wild*.

53. Mendoza-Denton, *Homegirls*, 180.

54. Latour, *Reassembling the Social*, 71, 75.

55. For a fascinating work by social psychologists that follows a similar approach, see Middletown and Brown, *Social Psychology*.

56. Wertsch, *Voices of Collective Remembering*, 25. Scholars have considered a plethora of such "cultural tools," practices, and mnemonic devices, including monuments, museums, textbooks, and websites (Conway, "New Directions," 443), embodiment and "affective resonance" (Stewart, *Dreaming and Historical Consciousness,* 2), ritual, possession, and, more recently, dreaming (Bloch, *From Blessing*; Cole, *Forget Colonialism?*; Connerton, *How Societies Remember*, 22; Lambek, *Weight of the Past*; Sahlins, *Islands of History*; Stewart, *Dreaming and Historical Consciousness*; Stoller, *Embodying Colonial Memories*).

57. The literature on the role of the past in language use is now vast; recent reviews include French, "Semiotics of Collective Memories"; Monaghan, "Expanding Boundaries."

58. Inoue, "What Does Language Remember?," 41.

59. French, "Semiotics of Collective Memories," 338.

60. Joutard, *Ces voix*; Portelli, *Death of Luigi Trastulli*.

61. Briggs, *Competence in Performance*.

62. Tonkin, *Narrating Our Pasts*, 3; Bauman, *Story, Performance, and Event*.

63. Ochs and Capps, *Living Narrative,* 3.

64. Ochs and Capps, *Living Narrative,* 24, 54, 26.

65. Da Col and Graeber, "Foreword," vii.

66. Ochs and Capps, *Living Narrative,* 33.

67. Ochs and Capps, *Living Narrative,* 46, 51.

68. Latour, *Reassembling the Social.*

69. Lassiter, "Collaborative Ethnography."

70. Smith, *Memories of 4th and Lehigh,* n.d.

71. Smith, *Colonial Memory.*

72. Latour, *Reassembling the Social.*

73. Bahloul, *The Architecture of Memory,* 4.

74. Pietikäinen and Dufva, "Voices in Discourses."

75. Conway, "New Directions," 443; Yow, *Recording Oral History,* 35–67.

2. The Language of Blight

1. Eileen Kenna, "'Lebanese Town' Now a State of Mind," *Easton Express,* January 2, 1983, A1.

2. Long-standing home of the Lenni Lenape, much of the area came under settler possession through the infamous "Walking Purchase" carried out by William Penn's sons in 1737.

3. Raup, "Pennsylvania-Dutch of Northampton County," 12.

4. Ethnic succession is also reflected in the rotating religious establishments: a Jewish synagogue at 321 Lehigh Street was purchased in 1915 by Italians, who tore it down to build St. Anthony's Church. Lebanese and Italians shared that church for a good dozen years until it became too small. When Italian Catholics moved their church to a new location, the Lebanese bought their old building and established Our Lady of Lebanon in it in 1930. See US Census, 1880, for Easton, Northampton County, PA.

5. Many blacks were members of a large extended family network who traced their ancestry to Aaron Hoff, who arrived in Easton in 1834. Aaron O. Hoff and his wife, Diana, were born in New Jersey around 1815 and 1820, respectively. See US Census, 1850 and 1860, for Northampton County, PA.

6. Trachtenberg, *Consider the Years,* 188–196. There were 341 Italians in Northampton County in 1900, 1,582 in 1910, and 3,723 in 1920 (Grifo and Noto, "History of Italian Immigration," 10–14).

7. Our Lady of Lebanon Maronite Catholic Church (Easton, PA), "History of the Easton Lebanese," http://www.mountlebanon.org/histeast.html, accessed April 3, 2006. New York City had become the center of this enterprise by the 1880s, and from there networks of suppliers and peddling

circuits spread out into other regions of the country (Naff, *Becoming American*).

8. Naff, *Becoming American*, 17.

9. Of the 112 people in the city identified in the 1920 census as "Assyrian" or from the "Syrian Arab Republic," 40 percent worked as peddlers, 28 percent were merchants selling dry goods or fruits, and the remaining 26 percent were laborers at local iron, steel, or hosiery mills. Of these people, 33 percent (thirty-five individuals) were born in Pennsylvania, all of whom were born after 1907.

10. Acting Street Sergeant Keller took ten other police officers with him to arrest a few individuals, suggesting that the authorities were preparing for the worst. *Easton Argus*, November 29, 1916, 1.

11. Our Lady of Lebanon Maronite Catholic Church, "History of Easton Lebanese"; US Census, 1930, for Easton, Northampton County, PA.

12. Black homeowners in 1930 included Walter Hall at 341 Lehigh Street and Aaron Good at 339 Lehigh Street. See 1930 US Census.

13. "'Difficult' Renewal Job Coming to End in Easton," *Allentown Morning Call*, July 18, 1973, 11.

14. Joint Planning Commission Lehigh-Northampton Counties, "Easton Central Business District" (research report, typescript, n.d.), 1, Planning and Redevelopment Archives, City Hall, Easton, PA.

15. *Annual Report of the City of Easton . . . 1958* (Easton, PA, 1959), 34.

16. Morris Knowles Incorporated to the Easton City Planning Commission, in *Annual Report of the City of Easton . . . 1957* (Easton, PA, 1958), 35.

17. Timothy Hare, "Governmental Role in the Decentralization of the Historic Area of Easton, PA from 1945 to 1960" (independent study project, Department of History, East Stroudsburg University, December 22, 1993, unpublished manuscript at Skillman Library, Lafayette College, Easton, PA), sec. 1, 55.

18. *Annual Report of the City of Easton . . . 1963* (Easton, PA, 1964), 67; Community Planning Subcommittee of the Citizens Advisory Committee, "Report on the Advisability of Including the Moose Property in the L-W Street Project" (typescript, March 23, 1965), Planning and Redevelopment Archives.

19. *Annual Report of the City of Easton . . . 1964* (Easton, PA, 1965), 76.

20. *Annual Report of the City of Easton . . . 1960* (Easton, PA, 1961), 45, 46.

21. *Annual Report of the City of Easton . . . 1961* (Easton, PA, 1962), 67.

22. *Annual Report of the City of Easton . . . 1962* (Easton, PA, 1963), 63. A reason given for the speed in clearing the land was the need for housing for the elderly.

23. "Council, Planners Due to Act by Wednesday on Redevelopment Job," *Easton Express*, January 25, 1963, 1, 16.

24. "Letter Protests Plans to Tear Down Building," *Easton Express*, January 29, 1963, 1.

25. "Council Gets Protest on Plan to Demolish Historical Headquarters," *Easton Express*, January 30, 1963, 1.

26. "Museum Question Solution?," *Easton Express*, February 11, 1963, 6; "Museum to Be Spared under Private Housing Plan Offered to City," *Easton Express*, February 11, 1963, 1.

27. "Must Easton Lose Museum?," *Easton Express*, January 31, 1963, 6.

28. "Council Gets Protest," 1.

29. "Council Okays Lehigh-Washington Redevelopment: Vote Is Unanimous Despite Objections by Area Residents," *Easton Express*, June 27, 1963, 1, 20; "Owners Protest Prices Offered on Properties in L-W Project Area," *Easton Express*, September 11, 1963, 1, 20.

30. "Redevelopment Decision by Council May Not Be Reached for Month," *Easton Express*, May 29, 1963, 1.

31. "Redevelopment Decision," 1, 10.

32. "Major Challenge in Renewal," *Easton Express*, February 12, 1963, 6.

33. Joseph C. Dowell, "Decline of Cities—Heavy Price of Progress," *Easton Express*, May 25, 1963, 6; Dowell, "Third of Easton's Housing Units Unfit," *Easton Express*, May 27, 1963; "L-W Program's Value to the City," *Easton Express*, May 28, 1963; "D-Day for Easton's Renewal," *Easton Express*, May 31, 1963, 6; Edward P. Kennedy, "Can Council Face Renewal Challenge?," *Easton Express*, June 1, 1963, 6; Kennedy, "Why City Renewal in L-W Sector?," *Easton Express*, June 8, 1963, 6; Kennedy, "Attacks on Renewal Neglect the Truths," *Easton Express*, June 19, 1963, 6; "A Display of Political Courage," *Easton Express*, June 23, 1963, 6; Dowell, "In Renewal, Piecemeal Approach Can't Work," *Easton Express*, August 7, 1963.

34. Kennedy, "Why City Renewal in L-W Sector," 6.

35. "Council Okays Lehigh-Washington Redevelopment," 1, 20.

36. "Owners Protest Prices Offered on Properties in L-W Project Area," *Easton Express*, September 11, 1963, 1, 20; "Easton Groups Air Availability of Mortgage Funds for Residents Dislocated by Renewal Projects," *Easton Express*, October 31, 1963, 5.

37. *Annual Report . . . 1963*, 68.

38. "'Difficult' Renewal Job Coming to End in Easton," *Morning Call*, July 18, 1973, 11.

39. Gelfand, *Nation of Cities*, 11.

40. Gotham, "City without Slums," 292; Teaford, *Rough Road*.

41. Von Hoffman, "Study in Contradictions," 299; Gotham, "City without Slums," 294. Gotham ("City without Slums") highlights the role played by the real estate industry spokespersons affiliated with the National Association of Real Estate Boards (NAREB) and its research arm, the Urban Land Institute, which recommended that cities condemn the blighted areas near the Central Business District (CBD) and sell or lease the lands to private developers for rebuilding.

42. Easton Redevelopment Authority, "Questions and Answers on Urban Renewal" (typescript, March 31, 1963), 6, Planning and Redevelopment Archives.

43. Lindbloom and Farrah, *Citizen's Guide,* 26.

44. Morris Knowles, Inc., "Easton: Report on Review and Updating of Land Use Plan" (typescript, 1962), 26–27, Planning and Redevelopment Archives.

45. Morris Knowles, Inc., "Findings: Lehigh-Washington St. Substandard Survey" (typescript, n.d.), Planning and Redevelopment Archives.

46. *Annual Report . . . 1962,* 63.

47. Morris Knowles, Inc., "Easton: Report on Review," 28.

48. The *1960 U.S. Census of Housing* provided examples of slight defects: "lack of paint; slight damage to porch or steps; small cracks in walls . . . cracked windows." Housing that is "deteriorating" needs "more repair than would be provided in the course of regular maintenance" and is exemplified by "intermediate defects," such as "holes, open cracks, rotted, loose, or missing material over a small area of the foundation, walls, roof, floors or ceilings." Housing deemed "dilapidated" does not offer "safe and adequate shelter" and thus "endangers the health, safety, or well-being of the occupants." Such housing has at least one "critical" defect, or it has numerous "intermediate" defects that require the structure to be "extensively repaired, rebuilt, or torn down." *1960 U.S. Census of Housing,* vol. 1, *States and Small Areas* (Washington, DC, 1963), xxxii–xxxiii.

49. Morris Knowles, Inc., "Easton: Report on Review," 28.

50. *Annual Report . . . 1962,* 62–63.

51. Easton City Planning Commission, "A Report on the Comprehensive General Plan of the City of Easton, PA-1957" (unpublished bound report, 1957), 20, Planning and Redevelopment Archives.

52. "Minutes of the Council of the City of Easton, Pa.," June 27, 1963, p. 729, City Clerk's Office, City Hall, Easton, PA.

53. Former mayor, interview by Rachel Scarpato, July 11, 2007, Easton, PA.

54. "Population Characteristics" (typescript, Easton Community Renewal Program report no. 5, December 1964), 1, Planning and Redevelopment Archives.

55. "Minorities Group: A Research Report" (typescript report, Easton

Community Renewal Program report no. 8, August 1965), 2, Planning and Redevelopment Archives.

56. "Housing Conditions" (typescript, Easton Community Renewal Program report no. 10, August 1965), 18, Planning and Redevelopment Archives.

57. Mannion, "Lebanese Town."

58. The most highly rated neighborhood was new, racially homogeneous, and all white. Older neighborhoods that included Jews and working-class whites were next, and neighborhoods adjacent to African American neighborhoods were rated third. The fourth- and bottom-ranked neighborhoods were all African American ones. See FHA, *Underwriting Manual* (1936), 233, in Gotham, *Race, Real Estate*, 61.

59. Massey and Denton, *American Apartheid,* 19–31; see also Hirsch, "'Containment' on the Home Front"; Kaplan, *Urban Renewal*; Mollenkopf, *Contested City*; Sugrue, *Origins*, 48–50.

60. Gelfand, *Nation of Cities*, 213.

61. Weaver, *Negro Ghetto*, 324.

62. Gelfand, *Nation of Cities*, 213.

63. Morris Knowles, Inc., "Easton: Report on Review," 4, 7.

64. *United States Census of Population: 1960, General Social and Economic Characteristics* (Washington, DC, 1962), tables 21 and 25.

65. "Minorities Group," 3.

66. "NAACP Opposes Naming Moore to Authority Job," *Easton Express*, January 8, 1963, 5.

67. "Moore Presents Final Part of Gift to Easton," *Easton Express*, January 7, 1963, 12.

68. According to observer Turney T. Gratz, Easton Housing Authority's executive director, Thomas Bright also complained that 80 percent of the residences in the North Union Street redevelopment housing site had been occupied by African Americans before the buildings were razed and that the subsequent Jefferson Street project also affected more blacks than whites. Incensed by these allegations, and especially an *Easton Express* editorial that repeated the figures, Gratz reported that the black presence in the Union Street area had been 21 percent and that no blacks had lived on Jefferson Street. "High Rise Units to Be Known as 'Walter House,'" *Easton Express*, February 9, 1963, 1, 14.

69. "NAACP Opposes Naming Moore," 5.

70. "Moore Replies to Objections by NAACP Here," *Easton Express*, January 12, 1963, 5.

71. "Major Challenge in Renewal," *Easton Express*, February 12, 1963, 6.

72. "NAACP Branch Views Film on Urban Renewal," *Easton Express*, May 7, 1963, 5.

73. "Demonstration Here Planned by NAACP Unit," *Easton Express*, June 11, 1963, 7.

74. "Negroes Demonstrate, Claim Job Bias Here," *Easton Express*, June 15, 1963, 1.

75. "Easton Area Delegation Reaches Capital after Six-Hour Ride on Bus," *Easton Express*, August 28, 1963, 1, 20.

76. "Minorities Group," 2, 9.

77. The editorial states, "Slums—or 'blighted' areas, a fancy euphemism coined by planners and politicians to avoid ruffling feathers" (*Easton Express*, February 12, 1963, 6).

78. Former mayor, interview by Rachel Scarpato, July 11, 2007, Easton, PA.

79. Hugh Moore Jr., "Letter to the Editor," *Easton Express*, June 12, 1963, 5.

80. Birdwell-Pheasant and Lawrence-Zúñiga, "Introduction," 20.

81. Lindbloom and Farrah, *Citizen's Guide,* 181.

82. Gelfand, *Nation of Cities*, 208.

83. Gans, *Urban Villagers*; Mollenkopf, *Contested City*, 173–74.

84. Gordillo, *Landscapes of Devils*, 89.

85. For a description of Eastwick, see McKee, "Liberal Ends."

3. Narrating Diversity

1. Beissinger, "Occupation and Ethnicity"; Galaty, "Being 'Maasai.'"

2. Galaty, "Being 'Maasai'"; Larson, "Desperately Seeking"; Proschan, "'We Are All Kmhmu.'"

3. Proschan, "'We Are All Kmhmu,'" 93.

4. Trechter and Bucholtz, "White Noise," 8.

5. Hartigan, *Racial Situations*, 15.

6. Eriksen, *Ethnicity and Nationalism*, 174.

7. Proschan, "'We Are All Kmhmu,'" 91.

8. Hooglund, "Introduction," 3.

9. There were smaller numbers from Greek Orthodox, Melchite, and other churches. The 1920 census records indicated nearly fifty thousand "Syrians" living in the United States, but other sources suggest the number to be closer to two hundred thousand (Hitti, *Syrians in America*, 65).

10. Hooglund, "From the Near East," 88.

11. Baugh, "Politicization"; Fairchild, "Black, Negro"; Smitherman, "What Is Africa to Me?"; Thornton, Taylor, and Brown, "Correlates."

12. Baugh, "Politicization," 133; Smitherman, "What Is Africa to Me?," 118–24.

13. Baugh, "Politicization," 133.

14. Hill, *Everyday Language,* 20.

15. Dick and Wirtz, "Racializing Discourses," E2.

16. Anderson, "Justifying Race"; Hill, "The Voices"; Hill, "Language, Race"; Hill, *Everyday Language,* 128–55; Modan, "Jews and Ethnic Categorization"; Modan, *Turf Wars*; Trechter and Bucholtz, "White Noise," 16; Trechter, "White between the Lines"; Wortham et al., "Racialization."

17. Ochs, "Indexicality and Socialization"; Ochs, "Indexing Gender."

18. Ochs, "Indexicality and Socialization," 295.

19. Hill, "Intertextuality as Source," 114.

20. Dick and Wirtz, "Racializing Discourses," E4; see also Urciuoli, *Exposing Prejudice.*

21. De Fina, "Orientation."

22. Barth, "Introduction," 14.

23. Barth, "Introduction," 29.

24. Galaty, "Being 'Maasai,'" 2; see also Beissinger, "Occupation and Ethnicity."

25. It is probably no surprise that our speakers rarely used the term "ethnicity"; this is a relatively new term even in academic discourse, emerging in English-language dictionaries in the early 1970s (see Eriksen, *Ethnicity and Nationalism*, 4).

26. This way of speaking was not limited to Easton in the 1950s or 1960s. Errington ("Reflexivity Deflected," 662) notes a similar usage in Rock Creek, Montana, where "it is very difficult to avoid having an ethnic identity" and where he was frequently asked his "nationality." See also Inoue, "Japanese-Americans in St. Louis," 149. See Henri Diament for a decidedly prescriptive stance on popular American usage for "nouns and adjectives of nationality" ("Ethnonyms in American Usage," 197).

27. Bucholtz and Hall, "Language and Identity," 382.

28. Van Dijk, *Elite Discourse,* 126; De Fina, "Orientation," 145.

29. De Fina, "Orientation," 139.

30. Bucholtz and Hall, "Language and Identity," 382.

31. Bucholtz and Hall, "Language and Identity," 383, 384.

32. Gordillo, *Landscapes of Devils.*

33. Modan, *Turf Wars,* 148.

34. The ethnic labels could be viewed as "first-order indexicals" that connect a specific way of speaking to residents of a specific location that is located below the level of conscious awareness (Silverstein, "Indexical Order"; Modan, *Turf Wars,* 186n3).

35. Wortham et al., "Racialization."

36. See Hill, *Everyday Language*, 143.

37. Trechter and Bucholtz, "White Noise," 16.

38. Trechter and Bucholtz, "White Noise."

39. Trechter, "White Between," 24, 30.

40. Frankenburg, *White Women*; Modan, "Jews and Ethnic Categorization."

41. Modan, *Turf Wars*.

42. Modan, *Turf Wars*, 106–7.

43. Gotham, "Racialization," 301.

44. Gotham, "Racialization," 301.

45. Blommaert, "Grassroots Historiography," 11.

46. Sugrue, *Origins*, 22.

47. Sugrue, *Origins*, 211, 212.

48. Bourgois, "If You're Not Black," 122; Guglielmo, "Encountering the Color Line," 69; Hirsch, *Second Ghetto*; Kazal, *Becoming Old*, 81.

49. Dick and Wirtz, "Racializing Discourses," E4; see also Silverstein, "Linguistic Categories"; Urciuoli, *Exposing Prejudice*.

4. Voices from the Past

1. For "processes of identification," see Bucholtz and Hall, "Language and Identity," 382.

2. Ivanov, "Heteroglossia," 100. This concept has been extended by linguistic anthropologists, who now look at intertextuality (see Tedlock and Mannheim, *Dialogic Emergence*, 15), double-voicing (Tedlock and Mannheim, *Dialogic Emergence*, 16), interdiscursivity (Silverstein, "Axes of Evals"), entextualization (Silverstein and Urban, *Natural Histories*), and genre and intertextuality (Briggs and Bauman, "Genre, Intertextuality"). Taken to an extreme, every word can be described as "interindividual"; as Bakhtin wrote, the possibilities and perspectives "embedded in the word" "are essentially infinite" (Bakhtin, *Speech Genres*, 121, 120).

3. Bakhtin, "Discourse in the Novel," 290.

4. We used this term in the panel "Strategies and Performances of Temporal Heteroglossia," coorganized by Jacqueline Messing and Andrea Smith and held at the 2013 Annual Meeting of the American Anthropological Association. We thank Jacqui and fellow panelists Kathe Managan, Julia McKinney, Adam Harr, Ashley Stinnett, Evelyn Dean-Olmsted, Camilla Vasquez, Marco Jacquemet, Aurora Donzelli, Sarah Hillewaert, and Patricia Lange for their thought-provoking engagements with this theme.

5. Bakhtin, "Discourse in the Novel," 290, 291.

6. Pietikäinen and Dufva, "Voices in Discourses," 213.

7. Irvine, "Say When," 105.

8. Hendon, *Houses in a Landscape*, 79.

9. Basso, *Wisdom Sits*; Gordillo, *Landscapes of Devils*.

10. Parmentier, *Sacred Remains*, 11, 12.

11. See Brink-Danan, "Names That Show."

12. Bakhtin, "Forms of Time."

13. Silverstein, "Axes of Evals," 6.

14. Agha, *Language and Social Relations*, 321.

15. Silverstein, "Axes of Evals"; see also Lambek, "Sakalava Poiesis," 124n22; Lempert and Perrino, "Entextualization," 207.

16. Kroskrity, "Narrative Reproductions," 42; see also Eisenlohr, "Temporalities of Community"; Lempert, "Conspicuously Past"; Wirtz, "Enregistered Memory."

17. Perrino, "Chronotopes of Story," 92.

18. Goffman, *Frame Analysis*.

19. Briggs, *Competence in Performance*, 75.

20. For double voicing, see Heller, *Bilingualism*, 30; Bakhtin, "Forms of Time," 324. Don Gabriel's narrative is in Hill, "Voices of Don Gabriel," 117.

21. Dick, "Imagined Lives," 284, emphasis added.

22. See Dick, "Imagined Lives"; Hill, "Voices of Don Gabriel"; Goffman, *Forms of Talk*, 144.

23. Dick, "Imagined Lives," 284; see also Hill, "Voices of Don Gabriel."

24. Segal, "Cognitive-Phenomenological Theory," 64.

25. See Baugh, "Politicization"; Smitherman, "What Is Africa to Me?"

26. Baugh, "Politicization," 133; Smitherman, "What Is Africa to Me?," 118–24.

27. Bahloul, *Architecture of Memory*, 86, quote at 89.

28. Parmentier, *Sacred Remains*.

29. Williams, *Marxism and Literature*, 38; see also Inoue, "What Does Language Remember?," 41.

30. Dufva, "From 'Psycholinguistics,'" 88, 90, 92.

5. The Material of Memory

1. Halbwachs, *The Collective Memory*.

2. Hendon, *Houses in a Landscape*; Rasmussen, "Touching Materiality"; Renfrew, "Material Engagement."

3. Halbwachs, *The Collective Memory*, 129.

4. Parmentier, *Sacred Remains*, 11.

5. Rasmussen, "Touching Materiality," 124.

6. Parmentier, *Sacred Remains*, 12, emphasis added; see also Brink-Danan, "Names That Show."

7. Jones, *Memory and Material*; Basso, *Wisdom Sits*; Gordillo, *Landscapes of Devils*.

8. Halbwachs, *The Collective Memory*, 130.

9. Interview by Ashley Boyd and Travis Nicholson, February 27, 2014.

10. Bahloul, *Architecture of Memory*, 4.

11. Basso, *Wisdom Sits*, 5, 43, 42.

12. Interview by Miranda Wilcha, Sarah Geller, Jeannine Wagenbach, and Walter Burkat, March 11, 2014.

13. Interview by Dan DeSena and Sarah Woodruff, March 11, 2014.

14. Basso, *Wisdom Sits*, 10.

15. Halbwachs, *The Collective Memory*.

16. Feld, "Waterfalls of Song," 91.

17. Pred, *Place, Practice*, 6, 2.

18. Gell, *Art and Agency*, 85.

19. Connerton, *How Societies Remember*, 95.

20. Middletown and Brown, *Social Psychology*, 46–48.

21. Rasmussen, "Touching Materiality," 114, 119, 125, 123.

22. Hendon, *Houses in a Landscape*, 79, emphasis added, 80.

23. Hendon, *Houses in a Landscape*, 144.

24. Bachelard, *Poetics of Space*.

25. Birdwell-Pheasant and Lawrence-Zúñiga, "Introduction," 1.

26. Bourdieu, *Outline of a Theory*.

27. Hendon, *Houses in a Landscape*, 104.

28. Miller, "Behind Closed Doors," 12.

29. Hendon, *Houses in a Landscape,* 105, 124.

30. Myers, "Ways of Place-Making," 85, 87; see Myers, *Pintupi Country,* esp. chap. 5, for a more expanded discussion.

31. Pred, *Place, Practice, and Structure*, 17, 190, 20, 30, emphasis added.

32. This point, that "places gather," has been emphasized by anthropologists, cultural geographers, and philosophers such as Edward S. Casey, many of whom have been inspired by the work of phenomenologists like Martin Heidegger. See Casey, "How to Get," 24, and the excellent collection of essays edited by Feld and Basso, *Senses of Place*.

6. Nostalgia as Engine of Change

1. Bissell, "Engaging Colonial Nostalgia"; Smith, "Colonial Nostalgia"; Stewart, "Nostalgia, a Polemic."

2. Stewart, *A Space*, 7.

3. Nosco, *Remembering Paradise*, 5. See also Smith, "Place Replaced"; Smith, *Colonial Memory*; Stewart, *A Space*.

4. *Nóstos* (Greek, "return home") + *álgos* (Greek, "pain"), in Hofer, *Dissertation*. See also Stewart, "Nostalgia, a Polemic," 228; Lowenthal, *The Past*, 4. Lowenthal describes nostalgia as "the universal catchword for looking

back" and writes that it "now attracts or afflicts most levels of society" (*The Past*, 11).

5. Hofer, Dissertation; Bissell, "Engaging Colonial Nostalgia," 224.
6. Stewart, *A Space*, 227, 228.
7. Steve Armstrong, "The Appearance of Easton Is Irreversibly Changed," *Easton Express*, May 11, 1977.
8. The parishioners finally managed to secure some compensation from the Easton Redevelopment Authority and were granted a new building just opposite the boundary of the old Lehigh-Washington Street project, diagonally across from St. John's Lutheran Church, which had been spared in the redevelopment.
9. Armstrong, "Appearance of Easton."
10. Easton City Planning Commission's Annual Report for 1969 (typescript, March 24, 1970), 1, Planning and Redevelopment Archives.
11. Gordillo, *Rubble*, 82 (on capitalist exploitation), 81.
12. We cannot emphasize enough the significance of the former *economic order* for the evolution of the sociality our interlocutors emphasize, points stressed by William Julius William, *When Work Disappears*. See also Harvey, *The New Urbanism*, 23.
13. City of Easton, *Minorities Report*, 2, 9.
14. Hirsch, *Second Ghetto*; Massey and Denton, *American Apartheid*; Sugrue, *Origins*; Weaver, *Negro Ghetto*.
15. For "reportable," see Labov, *Black English Vernacular,* 370; for "tellable," see Ochs and Capps, *Living Narrative,* 33.
16. Gordillo, *Rubble*; Tsing, *Friction*; Berman, *All That Is Solid*.
17. Gordillo, *Rubble*, 81; Stoler, *Imperial Debris*.
18. Lefebvre, *Production of Space*, 53.
19. Stewart, *A Space*, 42.
20. Stewart, *A Space*, 42.
21. Bielo, "Promises of Place," 1.
22. There are too many texts to mention them all. Interested readers may wish to consult Bryant, *Past in Pieces*; Herzfeld, *Evicted from Eternity*; Bender and Winer, *Contested Landscapes*.
23. Sanders, "Urban Nomads," 267, 260, 265.
24. Halbwachs, *The Collective Memory*, 131, 134.
25. Otero, *La Calle*, 107–11, 103, 81.
26. Hartigan, *Racial Situations*, 13.
27. Saunders and Shackelford, *Urban Renewal*, 80–81.
28. Sogg and Wertheimer, "Legal and Governmental," 158–59, in Saunders and Shackelford, *Urban Renewal*, 65.

29. Saunders and Shackelford, *Urban Renewal*, 6.

30. Otero, *La Calle*, 143.

31. Otero, *La Calle*, 118–19.

32. Saunders and Shackelford, *Urban Renewal*, 80.

33. Hale, *Making Whiteness*, 10.

34. Stewart, *A Space*, 3.

35. Briggs, *Competence in Performance*, 59, 93.

36. Ochs and Capps, *Living Narrative*, 284.

37. Ochs and Capps, *Living Narrative*, 255.

38. See Stewart, *Dreaming and Historical Consciousness*, 1–9.

39. Bourdieu, *Theory of Practice*.

40. Durkheim, *L'évolution*, 16, quoted in Bourdieu, *Theory of Practice*, 79.

41. Tulving, "Episodic and Semantic Memory."

42. Mendoza-Denton, *Homegirls*, 180.

43. Rasmussen, *Touching Materiality*.

Bibliography

Abercrombie, Thomas A. *Pathways of Memory and Power: Ethnography and History among an Andean People*. Madison: University of Wisconsin Press, 1998.

Agha, Asif. *Language and Social Relations*. Cambridge: Cambridge University Press, 2007.

Alonso, Ana M. "The Effects of Truth: Re-presentations of the Past and the Imagining of Community." *Journal of Historical Sociology* 1, no. 1 (1988): 33–57.

Anderson, Benedict. *Imagined Communities: Reflections on the Origin and Spread of Nationalism*. London: Verso Press, 1991.

Anderson, Kate. "Justifying Race Talk: Indexicality and the Social Construction of Race and Linguistic Value." *Journal of Linguistic Anthropology* 18, no. 1 (2008): 108–29.

Appadurai, Arjun, ed. *The Social Life of Things: Commodities in Cultural Perspective*. Cambridge: Cambridge University Press, 1986.

Augé, Marc. *Non-places: An Introduction to an Anthropology of Supermodernity*. London: Verso Press, 1995.

Bachelard, Gaston. *The Poetics of Space*. Boston: Beacon Press, 1969.

Bahloul, Joëlle. *The Architecture of Memory: A Jewish-Muslim Household in Colonial Algeria, 1937–1962*. New York: Cambridge University Press, 1996.

Bakhtin, Mikhail. "Discourse in the Novel." In *The Dialogic Imagination. Four Essays*, edited and translated by Caryl Emerson and Michael Holquist, 259–422. Austin: University of Texas Press, 1981.

———. "Forms of Time and of the Chronotope in the Novel." In *The Dialogic Imagination: Four Essays*, edited and translated by Caryl Emerson and Michael Holquist, 84–258. Austin: University of Texas Press, 1981.

———. *Speech Genres and Other Late Essays*. Edited by Caryl Emerson and Michael Holquist. Translated by Vern W. McGee. Austin: University of Texas Press, 1986.

Barth, Frederik. Introduction to *Ethnic Groups and Boundaries: The Social*

Organization of Culture Difference. Edited by Frederik Barth, 9–38. Oslo,
    Norway: Universitetsforlaget, 1969.

Basso, Keith H. *Wisdom Sits in Places: Landscape and Language among the
    Western Apache.* Albuquerque: University of New Mexico Press, 1996.

Baugh, John. "The Politicization of Changing Terms of Self-Reference among
    American Slave Descendants." *American Speech* 66, no. 2 (1991): 133–46.

Bauman, Richard. *Story, Performance, and Event: Contextual Studies of Oral
    Narrative.* Cambridge: Cambridge University Press, 1986.

Bayor, Ronald H. "Another Look at 'Whiteness': The Persistence of Ethnicity
    in American Life." *Journal of American Ethnic History* 29, no. 1 (2009):
    13–30.

Beissinger, Margaret H. "Occupation and Ethnicity: Constructing Identity
    among Professional Romani (Gypsy) Musicians in Romania." *Slavic
    Review* 60, no. 1 (2001): 24–49.

Bielo, James S. "Promises of Place: A Future of Comparative U.S. Ethnogra-
    phy." *North American Dialogue* 16, no. 1 (2013): 1–11.

Birdwell-Pheasant, Donna, and Denise Lawrence-Zúñiga. "Introduction:
    Houses and Families in Europe." In *House Life: Space, Place and Family in
    Europe*, edited by Donna Birdwell-Pheasant and Denise Lawrence-Zúñiga,
    1–35. Oxford: Berg, 1999.

Bissell, William C. "Engaging Colonial Nostalgia." *Cultural Anthropology* 20,
    no. 2 (2005): 215–48.

Bloch, Maurice. *From Blessing to Violence: History and Ideology in the Circum-
    cision Ritual of the Merina.* Cambridge: Cambridge University Press, 1986.

Blommaert, Jan. "Grassroots Historiography and the Problem of Voice:
    Tshibumba's Histoire du Zaïre." *Journal of Linguistic Anthropology* 14, no. 1
    (2004): 6–23.

Bourdieu, Pierre. *Outline of a Theory of Practice.* Cambridge: Cambridge
    University Press, 1977.

Bourgois, Philippe. "If You're Not Black You're White: A History of Ethnic
    Relations in St. Louis." *City & Society* 3, no. 2 (1989): 106–31.

Boyarin, Jonathan. *Polish Jews in Paris: The Ethnography of Memory.* Bloom-
    ington: Indiana University Press, 1991.

Briggs, Charles L. *Competence in Performance: The Creativity of Tradition in
    Mexicano Verbal Art.* Philadelphia: University of Pennsylvania Press, 1988.

Briggs, Charles, and Richard Bauman. "Genre, Intertextuality, and Social
    Power." *Journal of Linguistic Anthropology* 2, no. 2 (1992): 131–72.

Brink-Danan, Marcy. "Names That Show Time: Turkish Jews as 'Strangers'
    and the Semiotics of Reclassification." *American Anthropologist* 112, no. 3
    (2010): 384–96.

Brodkin, Karen. *How Jews Became White Folks and What That Says about Race in America*. New Brunswick NJ: Rutgers University Press, 1998.

Brow, James. "Notes on Community, Hegemony, and the Uses of the Past." *Anthropological Quarterly* 63, no. 1 (1990): 1–5.

Bucholtz, Mary, and Kira Hall. "Language and Identity." In *A Companion to Linguistic Anthropology*, edited by Alessandro Duranti, 369–94. Malden MA: Blackwell Publishing, 2004.

Burke, Peter. "History as Social Memory." In *Memory: History, Culture and the Mind*, edited by Thomas Butler, 97–113. Oxford: B. Blackwell, 1989.

Casey, Edward S. "How to Get from Space to Place in a Fairly Short Stretch of Time: Phenomenological Prolegomena." In *Senses of Place*, edited by Steven Feld and Keith H. Basso, 13–52. Santa Fe NM: School of American Research Press, 1996.

Cole, Jennifer. *Forget Colonialism? Sacrifice and the Art of Memory in Madagascar*. Berkeley: University of California Press, 2001.

Conklin, Nancy Faires, and Nora Faires. "'Colored' and Catholic: The Lebanese in Birmingham, Alabama." In *Crossing the Waters: Arabic-Speaking Immigrants to the United States before 1940*, edited by Eric Hooglund, 69–84. Washington DC: Smithsonian Institution Press, 1987.

Connerton, Paul. *How Societies Remember*. Cambridge: Cambridge University Press, 1989.

Conway, Brian. "New Directions in the Sociology of Collective Memory and Commemoration." *Sociology Compass* 4, no. 7 (2010): 442–53.

Da Col, Giovanni, and David Graeber. "Foreword: The Return of Ethnographic Theory." *HAU: Journal of Ethnographic Theory* 1, no. 1 (2011): vi–xxxv.

De Fina, Anna. "Orientation in Immigrant Narratives: The Role of Ethnicity in the Identification of Characters." *Discourse Studies* 2, no. 2 (2000): 131–57.

DeMarrais, Elizabeth. "The Materialization of Culture." In *Rethinking Materiality: The Engagement of Mind with the Material World*, edited by Elizabeth DeMarrais, Chris Gosden, and Colin Renfrew, 11–22. Cambridge UK: McDonald Institute for Archaeological Research, 2004.

Diament, Henri. "Ethnonyms in American Usage: The Story of a Partial Breakdown in Communication." *Names* 29 (1981): 197–218.

Dick, Hilary Parsons. "Imagined Lives and Modernist Chronotopes in Mexican Nonmigrant Discourse." *American Ethnologist* 37, no. 2 (2010): 275–90.

Dick, Hilary Parsons, and Kristina Wirtz. "Racializing Discourses." *Journal of Linguistic Anthropology* 21, no. s1 (2011): E2–E10.

Dufva, Hannele. "From 'Psycholinguistics' to a Dialogical Psychology of

Language: Aspects of the Inner Discourse(s)." In *Dialogues on Bakhtin: Interdisciplinary Readings*, edited by Mika Lähteenmäki and Hannele Dufva, 87–104. Jyväskylä, Finland: University of Jyväskylä, 1998.

Durkheim, Émile. *L'évolution pédagogique en France*. Paris: Alcan, 1938.

Eisenlohr, Patrick. *Little India: Diaspora, Time, and Ethnolinguistic Belonging in Hindu Mauritius*. Berkeley: University of California Press, 2006.

———. "Temporalities of Community: Ancestral Language, Pilgrimage, and Diasporic Belonging in Mauritius." *Journal of Linguistic Anthropology* 14, no. 1 (2004): 81–98.

Epstein, Beth S. *Collective Terms: Race, Culture, and Community in a State-Planned City in France*. New York: Berghahn, 2011.

Eriksen, Thomas H. *Ethnicity and Nationalism*. Sterling VA: Pluto Press, 2002.

Errington, Frederick. "Reflexivity Deflected: The Festival of Nations as an American Cultural Performance." *American Ethnologist* 14, no. 4 (1987): 654–67.

Fairchild, Halford H. "Black, Negro, or Afro-American? The Differences Are Crucial!" *Journal of Black Studies* 16, no. 1 (1985): 47–55.

Feld, Steven. "Waterfalls of Song: An Acoustemology of Place Resounding in Bosavi, Papua New Guinea." In *Senses of Place*, edited by Steven Feld and Keith Basso, 91–135. Santa Fe NM: School of American Research Press, 1996.

Feld, Steven, and Keith H. Basso, eds. *Senses of Place*. Santa Fe NM: School of American Research Press, 1996.

Fourcade, Marie-Blanche. *Habiter l'Arménie au Québec*. Québec: Presses de l'Université du Québec, 2011.

Frankenburg, Ruth. *White Women, Race Matters: The Social Construction of Whiteness*. Minneapolis: University of Minnesota Press, 1993.

French, Brigittine. "The Semiotics of Collective Memories." *Annual Review of Anthropology* 41 (2012): 337–53.

Galaty, John G. "Being 'Maasai'; Being 'People-of-Cattle': Ethnic Shifters in East Africa." *American Ethnologist* 9, no. 1 (1982): 1–20.

Gans, Herbert J. *The Urban Villagers: Group and Class in the Life of Italian-Americans*. New York: Free Press, 1982.

Gelfand, Mark. *A Nation of Cities: The Federal Government and Urban America, 1933–1965*. New York: Oxford University Press, 1975.

Gell, Alfred. *Art and Agency: An Anthropological Theory*. Oxford: Oxford University Press, 1998.

Goffman, Erving. *Forms of Talk*. Philadelphia: University of Pennsylvania Press, 1981.

———. *Frame Analysis: An Essay on the Organization of Experience*. New York: Harper and Row, 1974.

Gordillo, Gastón R. *Landscapes of Devils: Tensions of Place and Memory in the Argentinean Chaco*. Durham NC: Duke University Press, 2004.

———. *Rubble: The Afterlife of Destruction*. Durham NC: Duke University Press, 2014.

Gotham, Kevin Fox. "A City without Slums: Urban Renewal, Public Housing, and Downtown Revitalization in Kansas City, Missouri." *American Journal of Economics and Sociology* 60, no. 1 (2001): 285–316.

———. *Race, Real Estate, and Uneven Development: The Kansas City Experience, 1900–2010*. Albany: State University of New York Press, 2014.

———. "Racialization and the State: The Housing Act of 1934 and the Creation of the Federal Housing Administration." *Sociological Perspectives* 43, no. 2 (2000): 291–317.

Grifo, Richard D., and Anthony F. Noto. *A History of Italian Immigration to the Easton Area*. Easton: Northampton Historical and Genealogical Society, 1964.

Gualtieri, Sarah. "Becoming 'White': Race, Religion and the Foundations of Syrian/Lebanese Ethnicity in the United States." *Journal of American Ethnic History* 20, no. 4 (2001): 29–58.

———. "Strange Fruit? Syrian Immigrants, Extralegal Violence and Racial Formation in the Jim Crow South." *Arab Studies Quarterly* 26, no. 3 (2004): 63–85.

Guglielmo, Thomas A. "Encountering the Color Line in the Everyday: Italians in Interwar Chicago." *Journal of American Ethnic History* 23, no. 4 (2003): 45–77.

———. *White on Arrival: Italians, Race, Color, and Power in Chicago, 1890–1945*. New York: Oxford University Press, 2004.

Gupta, Akhil, and James Ferguson. "Beyond 'Culture': Space, Identity, and the Politics of Difference." In *Culture, Power, Place: Exploration in Critical Anthropology*, edited by Akhil Gupta and James Ferguson, 33–45. Durham NC: Duke University Press, 1997.

Halbwachs, Maurice. *The Collective Memory*. 1950; New York: Harper and Row, 1980.

———. "Les expropriations et le prix des terrains à Paris, 1860–1900." Thesis, Faculté de Droit, l'Université de Paris, 1909.

———. *On Collective Memory*. Edited and translated by Lewis Coser. Chicago: University of Chicago Press, 1992.

Hale, Grace Elizabeth. *Making Whiteness: The Culture of Segregation in the South, 1890–1940*. New York: Vintage Books, 1998.

Harrison, Alferdteen. *Black Exodus: The Great Migration from the American South*. Jackson: University Press of Mississippi, 1991.

Hartigan, John, Jr. *Racial Situations: Class Predicaments of Whiteness in Detroit.* Princeton NJ: Princeton University Press, 1999.

Harvey, David. *The Condition of Postmodernity.* Oxford: Oxford University Press, 1989.

———. *Justice, Nature, and the Geography of Difference.* Oxford: Oxford University Press, 1996.

———. "The New Urbanism and the Communitarian Trap: On Social Problems and the False Hope of Design." In *Sprawl and Suburbia: A Harvard Design Magazine Reader*, edited by William S. Saunders, 21–26. Minneapolis: University of Minnesota Press, 2005.

Heller, Monica, ed. *Bilingualism: A Social Approach.* New York: Palgrave, 2007.

Hendon, Julia A. *Houses in a Landscape: Memory and Everyday Life in Mesoamerica.* Durham NC: Duke University Press, 2010.

Hill, Jane H. *The Everyday Language of White Racism.* Chichester UK: Wiley-Blackwell, 2008.

———. "The Voices of Don Gabriel: Responsibility and Self in a Modern Mexicano Narrative." In *The Dialogic Emergence of Culture*, edited by Dennis Tedlock and Bruce Mannheim, 97–147. Urbana: University of Illinois Press, 1995.

Hirsch, Arnold R. "'Containment' on the Home Front: Race and Federal Housing Policy from the New Deal to the Cold War." *Journal of Urban History* 26 (2000): 158–89.

———. "E. Pluribus Duo? Thoughts on 'Whiteness' and Chicago's 'New' Immigration as a Transient Third Tier." Special issue, "The Study of 'Whiteness,'" *Journal of American Ethnic History* 23, no. 4 (2004): 7–44.

———. *Making the Second Ghetto: Race and Housing in Chicago, 1940–1960.* New York: Cambridge University Press, 1983.

Hitti, Philip K. *The Syrians in America.* New York: George H. Doran Company, 1924.

Hobsbawm, Eric, and Terence Ranger, eds. *The Invention of Tradition.* Cambridge: Cambridge University Press, 1983.

Hofer, Johannes. "Medication Dissertation on Nostalgia, 1688." Trans. Carolyn Kiser Anspach. *Bulletin of the History of Medicine* 2 (1934): 376–91.

Holsey, Bayo. *Routes of Remembrance: Refashioning the Slave Trade in Ghana.* Chicago: University of Chicago Press, 2008.

Hooglund, Eric J. "From the Near East to Down East." In *Crossing the Waters: Arabic-Speaking Immigrants to the United States before 1940,* edited by Eric Hooglund, 85–102. Washington DC: Smithsonian Institution Press, 1987.

———. Introduction to *Crossing the Waters: Arabic-Speaking Immigrants to the United States before 1940,* edited by Eric Hooglund, 1–14. Washington DC: Smithsonian Institution Press, 1987.

Hoskins, Janet. "Agency, Biography and Objects." In *Handbook of Material Culture,* edited by Christopher Tilley et al., 76–83. Los Angeles: Sage Press, 2006.

———. *Biographical Objects: How Things Tell the Stories of People's Lives.* London: Routledge, 1998.

Hutchins, Edwin. *Cognition in the Wild.* Boston: MIT Press, 1995.

Ignatiev, Noel. *How the Irish Became White.* New York: Routledge, 1995.

Inoue, Miyako. "Japanese-Americans in St. Louis: From Internees to Professionals." *City & Society* 3, no. 2 (1989): 142–52.

———. "Temporality and Historicity in and through Linguistic Anthropology." *Journal of Linguistic Anthropology* 14, no. 1 (2004): 1–5.

———. "What Does Language Remember? Indexical Inversion and the Naturalized History of Japanese Women." *Journal of Linguistic Anthropology* 14, no. 1 (2004): 39–56.

Irvine, Judith. "Say When: Temporalities in Language Ideology." *Journal of Linguistic Anthropology* 14, no. 1 (2004): 99–109.

Irwin-Zarecka, Iwona. *Frames of Remembrance: The Dynamics of Collective Memory.* New Brunswick NJ: Transaction Publishers, 1994.

Ivanov, Vyacheslav. "Heteroglossia." *Journal of Linguistic Anthropology* 9, no. 1–2 (1999): 100–102.

Jacobson, Matthew F. *Whiteness of a Different Color: European Immigrants and the Alchemy of Race.* Cambridge MA: Harvard University Press, 1998.

Jones, Andrew. *Memory and Material Culture.* Cambridge: Cambridge University Press, 2007.

Joutard, Philippe. *Ces voix qui nous viennent du passé.* Paris: Hachette, 1983.

Judd, Dennis R. *The Politics of Urban Planning: The East St. Louis Experience.* Urbana: University of Illinois Press, 1973.

Kaplan, Harold. *Urban Renewal Politics: Slum Clearance in Newark.* New York: Columbia University Press, 1963.

Karpat, Kemal. "The Ottoman Emigration to America, 1860–1914." *International Journal of Middle East Studies* 17 (1985): 175–209.

Kazal, Russell A. *Becoming Old Stock: The Paradox of German-American Identity.* Princeton NJ: Princeton University Press, 2004.

Kopytoff, Igor. "The Cultural Biography of Things: Commoditization as Process." In *The Social Life of Things: Commodities in Cultural Perspective*, edited by Arjun Appadurai, 64–94. Cambridge: Cambridge University Press, 1986.

Kroskrity, Paul V. "Narrative Reproductions: Ideologies of Storytelling, Authoritative Words, and Generic Regimentation in the Village of Tewa." *Journal of Linguistic Anthropology* 19, no. 1 (2009): 40–56.

Kunstler, James. *The Geography of Nowhere: The Rise and Decline of America's Man-Made Landscape*. New York: Simon & Schuster, 1993.

Labov, William. *Language in the Inner City: Studies in the Black English Vernacular*. Philadelphia: University of Pennsylvania Press, 1972.

Lambek, Michael. "The Sakalava Poiesis of History: Realizing the Past through Spirit Possession in Madagascar." *American Ethnologist* 25, no. 2 (1998): 106–27.

———. *The Weight of the Past: Living with History in Mahajanga, Madagascar*. New York: Palgrave, 2002.

Larson, Pier M. "Desperately Seeking 'the Merina': Reading Ethnonyms and Their Semantic Fields in African Identity Histories." *Journal of Southern African Studies* 22, no. 4 (1996): 541–60.

Lassiter, Luke Eric. "Collaborative Ethnography and Public Anthropology." *Current Anthropology* 46, no. 1 (2005): 83–106.

Latour, Bruno. *Reassembling the Social: An Introduction to Actor-Network Theory*. Oxford: Oxford University Press, 2005.

Lefebvre, Henri. *The Production of Space*. Translated by Donald Nicholson-Smith. 1974; Oxford: Blackwell, 1991.

Lempert, Michael. "Conspicuously Past: Distressed Discourse and Diagrammatic Embedding in a Tibetan Represented Speech Style." *Language and Communication* 27 (2007): 258–71.

Lempert, Michael, and Sabina Perrino. "Entextualization and the Ends of Temporality." *Language and Communication* 27, no. 3 (2007): 205–11.

Lindbloom, Carl, and Morton Farrah. *The Citizen's Guide to Urban Renewal*. Rev. ed. West Trenton NJ: Chandler-Davis Publishing Company, 1968.

Low, Setha. "Spatializing Culture: The Social Production and Social Construction of Public Space." *American Ethnologist* 23, no. 4 (1996): 861–79.

Lowenthal, David. *The Past Is a Foreign Country*. Cambridge: Cambridge University Press, 1985.

Lund, Katrin Anna, and Karl Benediktsson. "Introduction: Starting a Conversation with Landscape." In *Conversations with Landscape*, edited by Karl Benediktsson and Katrin Anna Lund, 1–12. Surrey UK: Ashgate, 2010.

Mannion, Gainne. "Lebanese Town: Biography of a Neighborhood." Unpublished paper by Lafayette College student, December 20, 1980. Bureau of Planning Archives, n.d.

Massey, Doreen. *Space, Place, and Gender*. Minneapolis: University of Minnesota Press, 1994.

Massey, Douglas S., and Nancy A. Denton. *American Apartheid: Segregation and the Making of the Underclass*. Cambridge MA: Harvard University Press, 1993.

McKee, Guian. "Liberal Ends through Illiberal Means: Race, Urban Renewal, and Community in the Eastwick Section of Philadelphia, 1949–1990." *Journal of Urban History* 27, no. 5 (2001): 547–83.

Mendoza-Denton, Norma. *Homegirls: Language and Cultural Practice among Latina Youth Gangs*. Malden MA: Blackwell Publishing, 2008.

Meskell, Lynn. "Introduction: Object Orientations." In *Archaeologies of Materiality,* edited by Lynn Meskell, 1–17. Malden MA: Blackwell Publishing, 2005.

Middletown, David, and Steven D. Brown. *The Social Psychology of Experience: Studies in Remembering and Forgetting*. London: Sage Publications, 2005.

Miller, Daniel. "Behind Closed Doors." In *Home Possessions: Material Culture behind Closed Doors*, edited by Daniel Miller, 1–19. Oxford: Berg, 2001.

———. *Material Cultures: Why Some Things Matter*. Chicago: University of Chicago Press, 1998.

———, ed. *Materiality*. Durham NC: Duke University Press, 2005.

Modan, Gabriella Gahlia. *Turf Wars: Discourse, Diversity, and the Politics of Place*. Malden MA: Blackwell Publishing, 2007.

———. "White, Whole Wheat, Rye: Jews and Ethnic Categorization in Washington, D.C." *Journal of Linguistic Anthropology* 11, no. 1 (2001): 116–30.

Mollenkopf, John H. *The Contested City*. Princeton NJ: Princeton University Press, 1983.

Monaghan, Leila. "The Expanding Boundaries of Linguistic Anthropology: 2010 in Perspective." *American Anthropologist* 113, no. 2 (2011): 222–34.

Myers, Fred R. *Pintupi Country, Pintupi Self: Sentiment, Place and Politics among Western Desert Aborigines*. Berkeley: University of California Press, 1986.

———. "Ways of Place-Making." In *Culture, Landscape and the Environment: The Linacre Lectures,* edited by H. Fint and H. Morphy, 72–110. Oxford: Oxford University Press, 2000.

Myrdal, Gunnar. *An American Dilemma: The Negro Problem and Modern Democracy*. 1944; New York: Harper & Row, 1962.

Naff, Alixa. *Becoming American: The Early Arab Immigrant Experience*. Carbondale: Southern Illinois University Press, 1993.

Nosco, Peter. *Remembering Paradise: Nativism and Nostalgia in Eighteenth-Century Japan*. Cambridge MA: Council on East Asian Studies, Harvard University, 1990.

Ochs, Elinor. "Indexicality and Socialization." In *Cultural Psychology,* edited by J. W. Stigler, R. A. Shweder, and G. Herdt, 287–308. Cambridge: Cambridge University Press, 1990.

———. "Indexing Gender." In *Rethinking Context*, edited by Alessandro Duranti and Charles Goodwin, 335–58. Cambridge: Cambridge University Press, 1992.

———. "Stories That Step into the Future." In *Sociolinguistic Perspectives on Register*, edited by D. Biber and E. Finegan, 106–35. Oxford: Oxford University Press, 1994.

Ochs, Elinor, and Lisa Capps. *Living Narrative: Creating Lives in Everyday Storytelling*. Cambridge MA: Harvard University Press, 2001.

Otero, Lydia R. *La Calle: Spatial Conflicts and Urban Renewal in a Southwest City*. Tucson: University of Arizona Press, 2010.

Parmentier, Richard J. *The Sacred Remains: Myth, History and Polity in Belau*. Chicago: University of Chicago Press, 1987.

Perrino, Sabina. "Chronotopes of Story and Storytelling Event in Interviews." *Language in Society* 40 (2011): 91–103.

Petshek, Kirk R. *The Challenge of Urban Reform: Policies & Programs in Philadelphia*. Philadelphia: Temple University Press, 1973.

Pietikäinen, Sari, and Hannele Dufva. "Voices in Discourses: Dialogism, Critical Discourse Analysis and Ethnic Identity." *Journal of Sociolinguistics* 10, no. 2 (2006): 205–24.

Popular Memory Group. "Popular Memory: Theory, Politics, Method." In *Making Histories: Studies in History-Writing and Politics*, edited by Richard Johnson, 205–52. Minneapolis: University of Minnesota Press, 1982.

Portelli, Alessandro. *The Death of Luigi Trastulli and Other Stories: Form and Meaning in Oral History*. Albany: SUNY Press, 1991.

Pred, Allan. *Place, Practice and Structure: Social and Spatial Transformation in Southern Sweden, 1750–1850*. Cambridge: Polity Press, 1986.

Price, Richard. *First-Time: The Historical Vision of an Afro-American People*. Baltimore MD: Johns Hopkins University Press, 1983.

Pritchett, Wendell. "Race and Community in Postwar Brooklyn: The Brownsville Neighborhood Council and the Politics of Urban Renewal." *Journal of Urban History* 27, no. 4 (2001): 445–70.

Proschan, Frank. "'We Are All Kmhmu, Just the Same': Ethnonyms, Ethnic Identities, and Ethnic Groups." *American Ethnologist* 24, no. 1 (1997): 91–113.

Raffaetà, Roberta, and Cameron Duff. "Putting Belonging into Place: Place Experience and Sense of Belonging among Ecuadorian Migrants in an Italian Alpine Region." *City and Society* 25, no. 3 (2013): 328–47.

Rasmussen, Lisa Rosén. "Touching Materiality: Presenting the Past of Everyday School Life." *Memory Studies* 5, no. 2 (2012): 114–30.

Raup, H. F. "The Pennsylvania-Dutch of Northampton County: Settlement

Forms and Culture Pattern." *Bulletin of the Geographical Society of Philadelphia* 36 (1938–39): 1–16.

Renfrew, Colin. "Towards a Theory of Material Engagement." In *Rethinking Materiality: The Engagement of Mind with the Material World*, edited by Elizabeth DeMarrais, Chris Gosden, and Colin Renfrew, 23–32. Exeter UK: McDonald Institute for Archaeological Research, 2004.

Rodman, Margaret C. "Empowering Place: Multilocality and Multivocality." *American Anthropologist* 94, no. 3 (1992): 640–56.

Roediger, David R. *The Wages of Whiteness: Race and the Making of the American Working Class*. London: Verso, 1991.

———. *Working toward Whiteness: How America's Immigrants Became White: The Strange Journey from Ellis Island to the Suburbs*. New York: Basic Books, 2005.

Sahlins, Marshall. *Islands of History*. Chicago: University of Chicago Press, 1985.

Sanders, Joshunda. "Urban Nomads." In *Homelands: Women's Journeys across Race, Place, and Time*, edited by Patricia Justine Tumang and Jenesha De Rivera. Emeryville CA: Seal Press.

Sassen, Saskia. *Expulsions: Brutality and Complexity in the Global Economy*. Cambridge MA: Harvard University Press, 2014.

Saunders, James Robert, and Renae Nadine Shackelford. *Urban Renewal and the End of Black Culture in Charlottesville, Virginia: An Oral History of Vinegar Hill*. Jefferson NC: McFarland, 1998.

Schuyler, David. *A City Transformed: Redevelopment, Race, and Suburbanization in Lancaster, Pennsylvania, 1940–1980*. University Park: Pennsylvania State University Press, 2002.

Segal, Erwin M. "A Cognitive-Phenomenological Theory of Fictional Narrative." In *Deixis in Narrative: A Cognitive Science Perspective,* edited by Judith Duchan, Gail Iruder, and Lynne Hewitt, 61–78. Mahwah NJ: Lawrence Erlbaum Associates, 1995.

Shadid, M., MD. "Letter to the Editor." *Syrian World* 1, no. 11 (1927): 47–48.

Silverstein, Michael. "Axes of Evals: Token versus Type Interdiscursivity." *Journal of Linguistic Anthropology* 15, no. 1 (2005): 6–22.

———. "Indexical Order and the Dialectics of Sociolinguistic Life." *Language and Communication* 23 (2003): 193–229.

———. "The Limits of Awareness." In *Linguistic Anthropology: A Reader*, edited by Alessandro Duranti, 382–401. Oxford: Blackwell, 2001.

———. "Shifters, Linguistic Categories, and Cultural Description." In *Meaning in Anthropology,* edited by Keith H. Basso and Henry A. Selby, 11–55. Albuquerque: University of New Mexico Press, 1976.

Silverstein, Michael, and Greg Urban, eds. *Natural Histories of Discourse.* Chicago: University of Chicago Press, 1996.

Smith, Andrea L. *Colonial Memory and Postcolonial Europe: Maltese Settlers in Algeria and France.* Bloomington: Indiana University Press, 2006.

———. "Mormon Forestdale." *Journal of the Southwest* 47, no. 2 (2005): 165–208.

———. "Place Replaced: Colonial Nostalgia and Pied-noir Pilgrimages to Malta." *Cultural Anthropology* 18, no. 3 (2003): 329–64.

———. "Settler Sites of Memory and the Work of Mourning." *French Politics, Culture, Society* 31, no. 3 (2013): 65–92.

Smith, Andrea, and Rachel Scarpato. "The Language of 'Blight' and Easton's 'Lebanese Town': Understanding a Neighborhood's Loss to Urban Renewal." *Pennsylvania Magazine of History and Biography* 134, no. 2 (2010): 127–64.

Smitherman, Geneva. "What Is Africa to Me? Language, Ideology, and African Americans." *American Speech* 66, no. 2 (1991): 115–32.

Stewart, Charles. *Dreaming and Historical Consciousness in Island Greece.* Cambridge MA: Harvard University Press, 2012.

Stewart, Kathleen. "Nostalgia: A Polemic." *Cultural Anthropology* 3, no. 3 (1988): 227–41.

———. *A Space on the Side of the Road: Cultural Poetics in an "Other" America.* Princeton NJ: Princeton University Press, 1996.

Stoler, Ann Laura. "The Rot Remains: From Ruins to Ruination." In *Imperial Debris: On Ruins and Ruination,* edited by Ann Laura Stoler, 1–35. Durham NC: Duke University Press, 2013.

Stoller, Paul. *Embodying Colonial Memories: Spirit Possession, Power, and the Hauka in West Africa.* New York: Routledge, 1995.

Sugrue, Thomas J. *The Origins of the Urban Crisis: Race and Inequality in Postwar Detroit.* Princeton NJ: Princeton University Press, 1996.

Swedenburg, Ted. *Memories of Revolt: The 1936–1939 Rebellion and the Palestinian National Past.* Minneapolis: University of Minnesota Press, 1995.

Teaford, Jon C. *The Rough Road to Renaissance: Urban Revitalization in America, 1940–1985.* Baltimore MD: Johns Hopkins University Press, 1990.

Tedlock, Dennis, and Bruce Mannheim, eds. *The Dialogic Emergence of Culture.* Urbana: University of Illinois Press, 1995.

Thornton, Michael C., Robert Joseph Taylor, and Tony N. Brown. "Correlates of Racial Label Use among Americans of African Descent: Colored, Negro, Black, and African American." *Race and Society* 2, no. 2 (2000): 149–64.

Tonkin, Elizabeth. *Narrating Our Pasts: The Social Construction of Oral History.* Cambridge: Cambridge University Press, 1992.

Trachtenberg, Joshua. *Consider the Years: The Story of the Jewish Community of Easton, 1752–1942*. Easton PA: Centennial Committee of Temple Brith Sholom, 1944.

Trechter, Sara. "White between the Lines: Ethnic Positioning in Lakhota Discourse." *Journal of Linguistic Anthropology* 11, no. 1 (2001): 22–35.

Trechter, Sara, and Mary Bucholtz. "White Noise: Bringing Language into Whiteness Studies." *Journal of Linguistic Anthropology* 11, no. 1 (2001): 3–21.

Tulving, Endel. "Episodic and Semantic Memory." In *Organization of Memory*, edited by Endel Tulving and Wayne Donaldson, 381–403. New York: Academic Press, 1972.

Urciuoli, Bonnie. "Discussion Essay: Semiotic Properties of Racializing Discourses." *Journal of Linguistic Anthropology* 21, no. s1 (2011): E113–E122.

——. *Exposing Prejudice: Puerto Rican Experiences of Language, Race, and Class*. Boulder CO: Westview Press, 1996.

——. "Skills and Selves in the New Workplace." *American Ethnologist* 35, no. 2 (2008): 211–28.

Van Dijk, Teun A. *Elite Discourse and Racism*. Newbury Park: Sage Publications, 1993.

von Hoffman, Alexander. "A Study in Contradictions: The Origins and Legacy of the Housing Act of 1949." *Housing Policy Debate* 11, no. 2 (2000): 299–326.

Weaver, Robert. *The Negro Ghetto*. New York: Harcourt Brace, 1948.

Wertsch, James V. *Voices of Collective Remembering*. New York: Cambridge University Press, 2002.

Williams, Raymond. *Marxism and Literature*. Oxford: Oxford University Press, 1977.

Wilson, William Julius. *When Work Disappears: The World of the New Urban Poor*. New York: Knopf, 1996.

Wirtz, Kristina. "Enregistered Memory and Afro-Cuban Historicity in Santería's Ritual Speech." *Language & Communication* 27, no. 3 (2007): 245–57.

Wortham, Stanton, Elaine Allard, Kathy Lee, and Katherine Mortimer. "Racialization in Payday Mugging Narratives." *Journal of Linguistic Anthropology* 21, no. s1 (2011): E56–E75.

Yow, Valerie R. *Recording Oral History: A Guide for the Humanities and Social Sciences*. Lanham MD: Altamira Press, 2005.

Zimmer, Basil. *Rebuilding Cities*. Chicago: Quadrangle Books, 1964.

Index

eminent domain, 2, 6, 41, 48, 140, 144, 145

ERA. See Easton Redevelopment Authority (ERA)

ethnic, as term of use, 74, 78, 80, 82, 86

ethnic diversity, 10, 61, 78, 81–82, 86, 136. *See also* integration

ethnicity: and blight, languages of, 52–55; homogeneity and, 135, 136; integration and, 1, 10, 11, 12, 138, 155n24; of religious institutions, 68; segregation and, 65–66, 68, 74, 135; statistics on, 10; in suburbs, 37, 136, 139, 143; as term of use, 74, 163n25; urban renewal projects and, 52–55, 134, 142–43, 167n8. *See also* ethnic diversity; ethnonyms; *specific ethnic groups*

ethnic labels: black-white binary and, 11, 85–86; class and, 63–64, 73–74, 82, 86; distinctions and, 63, 69, 73–74, 78–79, 81–82, 86; economics and, 76–79; integration and, 63, 64–65, 74–75, 76; meanings of, 72–75; nationalities and, 74; past in present and, 147, 149; past terms and, 90, 95–99, 104–5; place and, 2, 63–64, 74, 76, 86–87; as political act, 96; race and, 10–12, 74–75, 80–82; remembering and, 9, 86–87; space and, 79; story world and, 75; whiteness and, 82–83; whites and, 11, 80. *See also* ethnicity; ethnonyms; *specific ethnic groups*

ethnography, 1–2, 3. *See also* research and methodology

ethnonyms, 68–71, 86, 95. *See also* ethnicity; ethnic labels; *specific ethnic groups*

exonyms, 70, 72

expressions, outdated, 89, 90, 99, 103, 104. *See also* past terms

expulsion, 4, 5–6, 7, 140, 143; legacy of, 140, 143

Gans, Herbert J., 61

gatherings, 1–2, 8–9, *9*, 18, 23–26, *25*, 129–30, 147

Gelfand, Mark, 6, 60

geography, local, *33*, 115–21, *116*, 129

German Americans: community history and, 34, 37; distinctions and, 79; ethnic labels and, 11, 69, 74, 83; integration and, 12; past terms and, 99; segregation and, 68; Syrian Town history and, 34, 37

Gordillo, Gastón R., 71, 135, 138

Gotham, Kevin, 84

Graeber, David, 21

Greek Americans, 10, 69, 74, 162n9

habitus, 148–49

Halbwachs, Maurice, 16, 109, 112, 122, 129, 141

Hale, Grace Elizabeth, 145–46

Hall, Kira, 75, 78

Hare, Timothy, 43

Hartigan, John, Jr., 10, 11, 142–43

Hendon, Julia, 15, 92, 123, 125–27

heteroglossia: description of, 90, 105–6, 164n2; temporal, 91–92, 94, 96, 101, 104, 150

Hill, Jane, 73, 154n19

historical consciousness, 2

history: anthropology of, 92; and narration, 104–6; signs of and signs in, 2, 92, 104, 109–12, *111*

Hofer, Johannes, 132

past terms (*continued*)

104; power of, 105; remembering and, 2, 89–90, 103, 105–6; as signs of history, 2, 93, 104; story world and, 97; Syrians and, 95–97, 98, 99; temporal heteroglossia and, 91–92, 94, 96, 101, 104, 150. *See also* expressions, outdated

paths, 13–14, 15, 123, 125, 128, 129. *See also* projects

pedagogical discourse, *146*, 147

Perrino, Sabina, 94

personhood, 82, 94, 96, 137–38, 150

Peters, Father Norman, 45–46

place: anthropology of, 7, 13, 166n32; and blight, languages of, 1–2; childhood activities and, 15, 122–24, 128–29; chronotope and, 111–12, 129; community and, 112, 127–30, 166n32; ethnic labels and, 2, 63–64, 74, 76, 86–87; ethnography and, 1; and geography, local, *33*, 115–21, *116*, 129; images of, 24–25, 27–29, *28*, 107, *108*, 109, *109*, 129; language and, 1–2, 14, 91, 128; materiality and, 13, 92, 113–15; multilocal, 13; non-place versus, 5, 6, 138–40; past in present and, 149–50; past terms and, 2, 90, 92–93, 104, 106; power and, 2, 13, 14, 29, 112; as process, 13–16; projects and, 15, 124–25, 128; remembering and, 2, 109, 113–15, 150

place-in-time, 93, 94, 101, 150. *See also* chronotope

place-loss, 1, 3–4, 7, 61, 140–43

place-making practices, 13, 61, 115, 127

place-names: past in present and, 149, 150; past terms and, 99–101, 104;

remembering and, 113–15, 121; space and, 150; Syrian Town and, 12, 155n27; time and, 150

political acts: collective remembering as, 16–17; community as, 16–17; ethnic labels as, 96; ethnonyms as, 71; past in present as, 146; remembering as, 22, 30; space and, 13; urban renewal projects and, 39, 53–54, 61, 142–43

poverty, in narratives, 76–78, 125

power: collective remembering and, 16–17; images of place and, 107; materiality and, 16, 93, 126; of past terms, 105; place and, 2, 13, 14, 29, 112; space and, 61, 105; urban renewal projects and, 48, 53, 57, 61, 79, 95; whiteness and, 86. *See also* agency, and past terms

Pred, Allan, 13–14, 15, 122–25, 128

projects, 13–14, 15, 124–25, 128. *See also* paths

Proschan, Frank, 69

race: and blight, languages of, 1–2, 55–59, 161n58, 161n68; class and, 11, 80–84; distinctions and, 79; ethnic labels and, 10–12, 74–75, 80–82; ethnography and, 1–2; ethnonyms and, 69–70, 86; indexicality and, 72, 73, 84; integration and, 1, 10, 11, 12; remembering and, 9, 16, 20, 145–46; urban renewal projects and, 53, 55–59, 142–43, 161n58, 161n68. *See also* blacks; whites

racial homogeneity, 17, 55, 83–84, 86, 132, 135–36, 138, 161n58

racialization, 12, 72. *See also* indexicality

Syrians (*continued*)
and, 12; past terms and, 95–97, 98, 99; population statistics and, 162n9; racial terms and, 12; as term of use, 70; whiteness and, 12. *See also* Lebanese Americans
Syrian Town: description of, 1, 6, 10; history of, 32–38, *35*, *36*, *38*, 157n2, 157n7; map of, *35*; as non-place, *5*, *6*, 138–40; place-names and, 12, 155n27

tellability, 21, 86
temporal heteroglossia, 91–92, 94, 96, 101, 104, 150. *See also* heteroglossia
terms from past era. *See* expressions, outdated; past terms
time (temporality): community and, 75; language and, 91; past in present and, 149–50; paths and, 13–14, 15, 125; place-in-time and, 93, 94, 101, 150; place-names and, 150; projects and, 13–14; suburbs and, 139. *See also* chronotope; past terms
"time-space" (chronotope). *See* chronotope; place-in-time; space; time
Title I of the Housing Act of 1949, 6, 48–49, 60
toponyms, 10, 12, 104, 150. *See also* Syrian Town
Trechter, Sara, 69, 82–83

Union Street project, 43, 161n68
urban renewal projects: Canal Street project and, 43; class and, 143; economics and, 132, 134–35, 143–46; eminent domain and, 2, 6, 41, 48, 140, 144, 145; ethnicities and, 52–55, 134, 142–43, 167n8; ethnography and, 1; history of, 6–7; Jefferson Street project and, 43; Lehigh-Washington Street project and, 41–47, *47*, 49, *51*, 52–60, 132, 134, 142, 158n22; narratives on, 38–40; place-loss and, 4, 7, 61, 140–43; place-making practices and, 61; political acts and, 39, 53–54, 61, 142–43; power and, 48, 53, 57, 61, 79, 95; race and, 53, 55–59, 142–43, 161n58, 161n68; remembering and, 31–32; Riverside Drive project and, *133*, 134; space and, 4, 138; Title I of the Housing Act of 1949 and, 6, 48–49, 60; Union Street project and, 43. *See also* blight, languages of

Von Hoffman, Alexander, 48

Wertheimer, Warren, 144
whiteness, 11, 69, 82–83, 84, 86. *See also* black-white binary; racism
whites: autonyms and, 72, 154n19; and blight, languages of, 161n58; class and, 11, 82–83; ethnic labels and, 11, 80; exonyms and, 72; integration and, 12; population statistics and, 10; racial homogeneity and, 138, 161n58; racial terms and, 10, 11, 69, 154n19; segregation and, 65, 66, 86; in suburbs, 142. *See also* blacks; race; whiteness
Wirtz, Kristina, 73
world: rebuilding a, 131–32, 146–51; and story world, 75–76, 97, 105, 149

In the Anthropology of Contemporary North America series:

Holding On: African American Women Surviving HIV/AIDS
Alyson O'Daniel

Rebuilding Shattered Worlds: Creating Community by Voicing the Past
Andrea L. Smith and Anna Eisenstein

To order or obtain more information on these or other University of Nebraska Press titles, visit nebraskapress.unl.edu.

CPSIA information can be obtained
at www.ICGtesting.com
Printed in the USA
LVOW07s0605190817
545582LV00003B/259/P

9 780803 290587